Best
TEA SHOP WALKS
in
WARWICKSHIRE

Julie Meech

Published by Sigma Leisure – an imprint of
Sigma Press, 1 South Oak Lane, Wilmslow, Cheshire SK9 6AR, England.

British Library Cataloguing in Publication Data
A CIP record for this book is available from the British Library.

ISBN: 1-85058-635-7

Typesetting and Design by: Sigma Press, Wilmslow, Cheshire.

Cover: Kenilworth Castle

Maps: based on sketch maps provided by the author

Photographs: Julie Meech

Printed by: MFP Design and Print

Disclaimer: the information in this book is given in good faith and is believed to be correct at the time of publication. No responsibility is accepted by either the author or publisher for errors or omissions, or for any loss or injury howsoever caused. Only you can judge your own fitness, competence and experience.

Acknowledgements

Grateful thanks are due to Paula Good, Assistant Press Officer at Ordnance Survey; David Hurry, Operations Director at Cambridge Coach Services; Dave Matthews, Commercial Officer at Stagecoach Midland Red; Jane Rollins, Public Relations Manager at National Express and Dr Andy Tasker, Director of Warwickshire Wildlife Trust. I should also like to thank Mrs J Harris, Rights of Way Enforcement Officer, and James Fretwell, Parish Paths Partnership Liaison Officer, both with Warwickshire County Council, for their prompt action in dealing with footpath problems.

Dedicated to Sheila, who provided good company on many of these walks.

This book has been compiled in accordance with the Guidelines for Writers of Path Guides published by the Outdoor Writers' Guild.

Map of Warwickshire, with main towns shown

Contents

Warwickshire

The American novelist Henry James is reputed to have said "Warwickshire is the core and centre of the English world; midmost England, unmitigated England." It's certainly true that this landlocked county lies at the very heart of England, and it has always been at the heart of things in other ways – few counties have played such a central part in our history. Many of those who helped shape our nation lived in Warwickshire or had their power base there, and some momentous events took place in the county. Think of Warwickshire and (if you can recall school history lessons) you think of people such as Ethelfleda ("Lady of the Mercians"), Simon de Montfort ("Father of the British Parliament") and Richard Neville ("Warwick the Kingmaker"); castles such as Kenilworth and Warwick; battles such as Edgehill. More famous than any of these, of course, is William Shakespeare, the man who really put Warwickshire on the map.

But though the lush green fields through which the Avon meanders are steeped in history, there are few visible signs of it in the countryside. Warwickshire is, now that Birmingham and Coventry have been detached from it, a largely rural area, mostly confined to the Midland plain, but also taking in just a little of the Cotswolds. The most notable feature of the plain is the valley of the River Avon, to the north-west of which is a countryside of scattered settlements, deeply-cut lanes and gentle hills which were once clothed by the Forest of Arden (not continuous forest, but a well-wooded area nonetheless). Even today, dense hedgerows still enclose the sheep pastures, small copses remain in secluded corners and statuesque oak trees punctuate the hedges or stand solitary in the fields. Sadly, the great elms – the "Warwickshire weed" – have long since fallen victim to Dutch elm disease. South of the Avon, the rich agricultural lands of south Warwickshire have been renowned for their fertility for centuries and the area is traditionally known as the Feldon, its prosperity reflected in the fine buildings which grace towns and villages such as Shipston and Brailes. Beyond the Feldon the land rises to the Cotswolds and, though Warwickshire's share is small, it is well worth seeking out.

While it may be mainly rural in flavour, the county does have busy towns, in which some of its long history is still plain to see. Stratford, Warwick and Leamington are the sort of towns which would grace any visitor's itinerary. All over the world the name of Stratford-upon-Avon is familiar because of the historical accident which made it the birthplace of William Shakespeare. Stratford is intrinsically attractive, but it is only the Shakespearean connection which has made it the second most popular tourist destination in Britain, beaten only by London. Many of those tourists then proceed to the great castles at Warwick and Kenilworth, but few penetrate any deeper. The countryside is virtually unknown, and even keen walkers have tended to pass it by, perhaps because there is nothing dramatic about Warwickshire, no striking geographical features, no mountains, no high hills, no turbulent rivers, nothing rugged or exciting. But if the hills are the merest bumps, at least they are easy to climb, and the views are enjoyable enough. This green and leafy, small-scale countryside, whose greatest asset is its sheer Englishness, has plenty to reward those who are willing to explore it in some detail.

The Tea Shops

Tea is seen as essentially English, but that's more to do with the fervour with which we have adopted it than with its origins. The story begins nearly 5000 years ago in China when, in the year 2750BC, a twig from a tea bush accidentally fell into Emperor Shen Nung's bowl of boiled water. Well, it's a nice story, and, true or not, tea is certainly Chinese in origin and didn't reach Europe until the 17th century. It was introduced by Portuguese and Dutch traders, and Charles II acquired a taste for it while exiled in the Netherlands. He was responsible for introducing it to Britain on his restoration to the throne in 1660, and so keen on it was he (or so valuable was it) that he accepted several cases of tea as part of the dowry when he married Catherine de Braganza, a Portuguese princess. Tea remained expensive, increasingly so after heavy taxation was introduced, leading to smuggling and black market trading, and it was many years before poorer people were able to afford it. Today, however, it is drunk by almost everyone in the British Isles, and with enormous enthusiasm by many. Despite the increasing popularity of coffee, tea is still seen as our national drink, and tea shops (all serving coffee too, of course,) abound throughout the country. Pubs are still far more common in rural areas, and this is especially true in Warwickshire, where it's rare to find a tea shop in a village. Most small market towns have at least one, however, often several, and there is almost always some sort of café or tea room at the craft centres, rare breed farms and other "attractions" which are so popular in today's countryside. All the tea shops in this book fulfil certain criteria and all have been visited by the author. They span a wide spectrum, but one thing they all have in common is a willingness on the part of their owners to be included in this book. You can be certain, therefore (barring a change of ownership), that walkers are welcome at all of these tea shops. However, please be considerate if wearing muddy boots and dripping waterproofs. Children are welcome at all of them too, but dogs are not generally permitted. There are some exceptions to this rule and where this is the case it is specified in the individual entry. Smoking is permitted at a few, and these are also specified. Opening hours are given for each tea shop but these can be flexible so it may be advisable to check in advance (telephone numbers are given) if you want to be sure that a particular tea shop will be open. Almost all of the tea shops cater for vegetarians to some extent, however limited. Some details are given with each individual entry but strict vegetarians are advised to ask for further information.

The Walks

None of the walks in this book is particularly demanding for most averagely fit people, and most are very gentle indeed. It's still as well to be properly equipped, although there's no need to invest your life savings in state-of-the-art gear. Common sense is the best guide, which means taking waterproofs with you, and sufficient layers of warm clothing in winter. It's best not to wear jeans if rain threatens as they're uncomfortable when wet and very slow to dry. Proper walking boots are by no means essential for all the walks in this book, but they do provide good ankle support, and they keep your feet dry in wet or muddy conditions (almost all the walks are potentially very muddy in winter). A small rucksack is the best way of carrying spare gear and you can get an adequate one for a few pounds.

Ordnance Survey maps are invaluable. The directions in this book should ensure you don't get lost, but maps enable you to make changes to the given route, to identify distant hills and to put the local scene in context. Landranger maps are ideal for an overview, while the more detailed Pathfinders and Explorers are superb companions on any walk. With a bit of practice you can learn to read a map almost like a book, building up a surprisingly accurate mental picture of an area before you've even set foot in it. Maps help you to interpret the landscape, identifying indeterminate humps and bumps as prehistoric cultivation terraces or deserted medieval villages, and they make route-finding easy, even showing which side of a hedge a footpath runs. The Pathfinder series is currently being replaced by the new Explorers, each of which covers a larger area and represents tremendous value for money. The first Warwickshire ones should be available quite soon. There is also an Outdoor Leisure map (at the same scale as the Pathfinders and Explorers) for the Cotswolds, and this includes quite a large chunk of south Warwickshire.

The directions given in this book should enable you to complete the walks without any difficulty, but bear in mind that things do change in the countryside – trees get blown over, hedges get ripped out, stiles get moved and cottages get knocked down. Any of these can make the directions invalid, but many paths are now waymarked (yellow arrows for footpaths, blue for bridleways) and are fairly easy to follow. Please note that where the directions indicate something along the lines of "climb a stile and go diagonally right", this assumes that, having climbed over the stile, you are standing with your back to it.

Any obstructions or other footpath problems should be reported (with grid references, if possible) to: The Rights of Way Officer, Department of Planning, Transport and Economic Strategy, Warwickshire County Council, PO Box 43, Shire Hall, Warwick CV34 4SX.

Long-distance Paths

Long-distance paths and other specially designated and waymarked routes have proliferated in recent years. All the routes listed below are encountered, however briefly, in the walks described in this book, so a short summary may be helpful.

The Arden Way: 25 miles/40km; a meandering, circular route in the area once covered by the Forest of Arden, based on the historic small towns of Henley-in-Arden and Alcester.

The Centenary Way: 100 miles/160km; Warwickshire's very own long-distance path, this linear walk from Kingsbury Water Park in the north to Meon Hill in the south was designed to reflect the history, culture, landscape and nature of the county. It connects with the Heart of England Way at both ends and was established in 1989 to mark the centenary of Warwickshire County Council.

The Heart of England Way: 100 miles/160km; a linear walk from Milford on the edge of Cannock Chase to Bourton-on-the-Water in the Gloucestershire Cotswolds. It skirts the eastern edges of the Black Country and Birmingham, passes through Warwickshire and then south across the Vale of Evesham to the Cotswolds. It connects the Staffordshire Way at Milford with the Oxfordshire Way at Bourton and also links up with a variety of other long-distance paths, such as the Cotswold Way and the Centenary Way.

The Macmillan Way: 290 miles/464km; a coast-to-coast linear walk following the limestone belt through ten counties from Boston in Lincolnshire to Abbotsbury in Dorset. Dedicated to the memory of Douglas Macmillan, the founder of the organisation now known as Macmillan Cancer Relief, it was developed to increase public awareness and to assist in fund-raising.

The Monarch's Way: 610 miles/976km; a linear walk (by an indirect route) from Worcester to Shoreham, which attempts to trace the approximate route taken by Charles II when fleeing from defeat at the Battle of Worcester in 1651.

Countryside Stewardship

In the course of some of the walks in this book, you will encounter areas of land which are part of the Countryside Stewardship scheme. Administered by the Ministry of Agriculture, this offers payments to farmers and landowners to enhance and conserve landscapes, wildlife and ancient monuments. Agreements usually run for 10 years, and while public access is not a requirement, it is encouraged. All the stewardship sites you will discover while doing these walks have public access and you are free to explore them. At the entry point to each site there are notices and detailed maps showing permitted access areas and footpaths.

Warwickshire Wildlife Trust

The Trust is the leading local environmental charity and one of 47 independent charities which form a national partnership – the Wildlife Trusts – with over a quarter of a million members and 2000 nature reserves throughout the UK. Warwickshire Wildlife Trust aims to protect wildlife and natural habitats throughout the county (and also Coventry and Solihull) and to encourage a greater awareness, appreciation of and participation in all aspects of nature conservation and the environment. The Trust has over 50 nature reserves, protecting areas of woodland, meadow and wetland. It campaigns for wildlife and the environment, helping to protect threatened places and rare species; it encourages people to enjoy nature by organising walks, talks and other events; it works with schools and community groups to support local action for the environment, and promotes ways for volunteers to help with practical projects and local activities. To join, or for further information, contact WWT at:

Brandon Marsh Nature Centre, Brandon Lane, Coventry CV3 3GW. (Telephone: 01203 302912. Website: www.wildlifetrust.org.uk; E-mail: warkswt @ cix.compulink.co.uk). As a member you will receive *Warwickshire Wildlife*, the Trust's own magazine, three times a year, and *Natural World*, the national magazine produced for all members of the Wildlife Trusts, also three times a year. Other benefits include free entry to Brandon Marsh Nature Centre, and to over 50 nature reserves, as well as membership of a local group and information about walks, talks and events.

Tourist Information Centres

Coventry: telephone 01203 832303/4.

Kenilworth: telephone 01926 52595/50708.

Leamington Spa: telephone 01926 311470.

Nuneaton: telephone 01203 384027.

Rugby: telephone 01788 535348.

Solihull: telephone 0121 704 6130/4.

Stratford-upon-Avon: telephone 01789 293127.

Warwick: telephone 01926 492212.

Public Transport

Surely all country walkers must have noticed that it's now almost impossible, in England and Wales, to escape the sound of traffic? Or to find a view unspoilt by cars? Or a village not choked by them? And who has not gone back to somewhere they once loved, only to find it no longer exists, but has been replaced by a huge swathe of tarmac bypassing some traffic-battered little country town? With the Countryside Commission predicting a doubling, or even trebling, of rural traffic, things can only get worse. People talk of spending time in the countryside to find "peace and quiet" and to "get away from it all" and yet they go there by car, thereby helping to destroy the very thing they're in search of, and providing ammunition for the arguments of those who would build yet more bypasses.

The problem is as serious in Warwickshire as anywhere else. As early as 1976, the author Lyndon F. Cave was describing the county as "The Motorway Hub of England" in his *Warwickshire Villages*. Since that time the construction of the M40 has sliced through what was previously one of the most beautiful and peaceful parts of the county, and innumerable bypasses have proved that a road doesn't have to be labelled a motorway before it's big enough, ugly enough and noisy enough to dominate a wide area of countryside. But, as even the Department of Transport has admitted, new roads generate new traffic, and congestion keeps on increasing. Stratford-upon-Avon has a population of just 23 000 but attracts 3.8 million tourists a year – an intake of about 11 000, almost half its own population, every day. Imagine the congestion and chaos if they all came by car. Sadly, rather a lot of them do, and then they wonder why the Stratford experience isn't quite what they expected.

It doesn't have to be that way. It's easy, cheap and fun to get around by public transport, and that's how all the walks in this book were accessed. Some services are excellent, some are undoubtedly poor, but overall the situation is improving, with innovative bus companies such as Stagecoach constantly adding new routes or upgrading existing ones. But in the long term it's up to us. If we use public transport, the demand will stimulate improvements. If we don't use it, we'll lose it.

Information about services is easily obtained. Warwickshire County Council has a telephone enquiry line and publishes free timetable books which cover the county, area by area. Monthly updates are also published and are obtainable from libraries, tourist information centres, Stagecoach Midland Red travel shops, other bus operators and council offices. Individual bus operators have their own enquiry lines and publish their own timetables. In addition, many libraries, tourist information centres, travel shops and rail stations have copies of the *National Express Timetable* and the *Great Britain Bus Timetable* (published by Southern Vectis Bus Company,

Nelson Road, Newport, Isle of Wight PO30 1RD. Telephone 01983 522456).

Information about public transport is given for each walk in this book, but some of the less useful bus services have been omitted for reasons of space. If you consult timetables you may find additional services. It's also worth remembering that services can change at short notice (several new ones have been introduced over the few months this book has been in production) so it's best to check the details before travelling. Do investigate the vast range of bargain fares available, especially from Stagecoach Midland Red. These include special day return fares, Explorer tickets giving a day's unlimited travel and a range of weekly and monthly passes which offer tremendous value for money. Changes in train ticketing arrangements take place frequently and integrated bus and train tickets are on the increase so it's a good idea to check out the promotional literature at your local station from time to time. One such integrated travel ticket is the recently introduced 'Shakespeare Country Explorer' available from Thames Trains. It allows one return journey between London and Stratford-upon-Avon and unlimited travel on Stagecoach Midland Red Buses and on trains between Leamington Spa, Warwick and Stratford. Available in 3-day and 5-day versions, it may be bought at London Paddington or by telephoning 0345 300 700. Don't think only in terms of local buses or trains for local travel. National Express, for instance, is usually perceived solely as a long-distance operator, but it's also useful for local travel within Warwickshire, while Cambridge Coach Services has several Warwickshire stops on its thrice-daily (each way) Cambridge to Worcester route (no pre-booking required).

Useful Phone Numbers for Public Transport Information

Warwickshire Traveline (8.30am-5.30pm Monday to Thursday, 8.30am-5.00pm Fridays): 01926 414140

National Express (8.00am-10.00pm daily): 0990 808080

National Rail Enquiries (24 hours): 0345 484950

TBC (Train, Bus and Coach) Hotline (6.00am-9.00pm daily): 0891 910910

Stagecoach Midland Red Busline (8.00am-6.00pm Monday to Saturday): 01788 535555

Cambridge Coach Services (office hours): 01223 423900

Walk 1: Warwick and Old Milverton

Start/finish: Castle Hill, Warwick; grid reference 284650.

Summary: An effortless circular walk on the edge of Warwickshire's county town, using footpaths by the River Avon to visit the pleasant hamlets of Old Milverton and Guy's Cliffe. Though popular with local people, this attractive walk is rarely discovered by visitors to Warwick.

Length: 4½ miles/7.2km.

Maps: OS Landranger 151, OS Pathfinder 976.

Buses/Coaches: Stagecoach Midland Red X16 and X18 Stratford to Coventry via Warwick, daily; 19/19A Stratford and/or Hampton Magna to Bishops Tachbrook via Warwick, Monday to Saturday; 61 Lowsonford to Leamington via Warwick, Wednesdays and Saturdays; 66 Leamington to Warwick, every few minutes Monday to Saturday; Johnsons of Henley 62 Leamington to Solihull via Warwick, Wednesdays and Fridays; A Line Travel 539 Coventry to Warwick, Monday to Saturday; Cambridge Coach Services 71 Bromsgrove and/or Worcester to Cambridge via Warwick, daily; National Express 337 Brixham to Coventry via Warwick, daily; 460 Stratford to London via Warwick, daily; 480 Kidderminster to London via Warwick, daily; Flightlink 210 Wolverhampton to Gatwick also operates via Warwick daily but stops only at the Little Chef on the A46.

Trains: Central Trains Leamington to Stratford and Leamington to Worcester via Warwick, daily; Chiltern Railways Birmingham to London via Warwick, daily; Thames Trains London to Stratford via Warwick, daily.

Parking: Public car parks in Warwick.

The Tea Shop
Meeting Point, Castle Hill, Warwick.

Owned by Castle Hill Baptist Church, this bright and sunny café, with fresh flowers on all the tables, is popular with locals and has a friendly, relaxed atmosphere. Run by volunteers, it makes donations to charities. As well as providing meals, Meeting Point also sells Fair-Trade goods from companies such as Traidcraft. Sales of such goods directly benefit their Third World producers. There are books for sale, too, and browsers are welcome. There is a very wide range of food on offer, including hot lunches such as lasagne, quiche, jackets and egg dishes, alongside the usual snacks and baked goods, as well as soups, ploughman's, salads and puddings. All-day breakfasts are also available and a good range of hot and cold drinks, including a selection of fruit teas. Cakes are home-made, and many vegetarian options are available. Dogs are welcome but must be left in the foyer.

Open: 10.30am-4.30pm Tuesday to Saturday. Closed Christmas week. Telephone: 01926 419393.

Mill Street, Warwick

The Walk

Warwick is one of our loveliest county towns. It was probably founded early in the Saxon era but then destroyed by the Danes. Ethelfleda, Alfred the Great's daughter, restored it and built a fortress in the 10th century. The first Earl of Warwick was Rohand, but it was the first post-Conquest holder of the earldom, Henry de Newburgh, who began the present castle. Later earls came from such famous families as the Beauchamps, the Nevilles, the Dudleys and the Grevilles, and thanks to their activities Warwick has a fascinating history – visit the castle or do some background reading to find out more.

Comparatively few medieval buildings survive in Warwick, which was devastated by a great fire in 1694, but those that do remain mingle happily with the newer ones of brick and stone which were built after the fire. Most of these Queen Anne and Georgian buildings are of great elegance, contrasting with a few modern horrors which have defaced the old townscape in recent years.

From Meeting Point at the top of Castle Hill, make your way down the hill. As you approach Castle Bridge you will see a footpath on the left, but first continue across the bridge for the classic view of the castle. Dramatically sited on a cliff above the Avon, Warwick is claimed to be the finest medieval castle in England, and has few

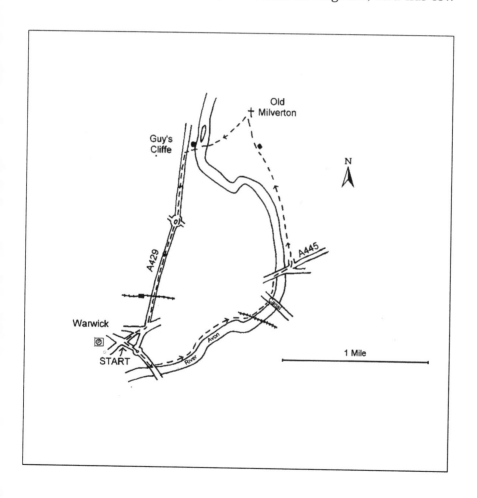

equals in the whole of Europe. Sadly, it no longer belongs to the Earls of Warwick.

Returning to the footpath, which is part of the Centenary Way, you'll find steps leading down into St Nicholas Park, a pleasant green space bordered by the River Avon, which you should follow towards Leamington.

Before long, you'll pass under an iron railway bridge and then under a stone aqueduct which carries the Grand Union Canal over the river. The path eventually climbs to a road bridge. Turn right beside the road, soon crossing and forking left to go along Rugby Road (A445) for a little way.

Turn left at Rock Mill Lane. When you reach Rock Cottage, fork right on a footpath which climbs gently, going high above the Avon, then descends again to cross a small tributary stream before continuing along the edge of a field. When it forks, stay on the higher path, with scrubby woodland on your left. At a path junction bear right on a well-trodden path towards a farm. At a waymarked post turn left to pass in front of the farm.

Across the river you can see Guy's Cliffe, where a 15th-century chapel and ruined 18th-century mansion stand beside the river. This is the place where the legendary Guy, a Saxon Earl of Warwick, lived out his last years as a hermit. The chapel was built for Richard Beauchamp and incorporates a statue of Guy, carved out of the rock against which the chapel stands. Unfortunately, there is no public access.

Pass the entrance to Manor Farm and continue to a gnarled, old walnut tree sheltering a waymarked gatepost. There is a choice of paths, but the most pleasant is the one that bears right towards the church at Old Milverton. A kissing gate and stile give access to the churchyard, burial place of Dr Jephson, of Leamington fame (see Walk 5). Go to the far left corner, where a gate gives access to a path leading across the fields towards the Avon. Two stiles and a footbridge take you across a silted-up channel of the river and a section of old, paved road to another footbridge spanning the Avon. There is a good view from here of the ruined house at Guy's Cliffe.

Go past an old mill, known as Saxon Mill but built in 1822 on the site of an earlier one, and now a restaurant. Keep straight on to reach the road and turn left on a footway, soon joining the Centenary Way which, for want of a more satisfactory alternative, simply follows the road into Warwick.

Walk 2: Warwick and Wedgnock Park

Start/finish: High Street, Warwick; grid reference 281646.

Summary: An easy circular walk which explores a stretch of the Grand Union Canal and an area of farmland which was once a deer park enclosed in the Middle Ages by the Earl of Warwick. As the route is mainly on bridleways there is only one stile to climb.

Length: 6½ miles/10.5km.

Maps: OS Landranger 151, OS Pathfinder 976.

Buses/Coaches: See Walk 1.

Trains: See Walk 1.

Parking: Public car parks in Warwick.

The Tea Shop

Quaker Community Café, 39 High Street, Warwick.

This attractive café is to be found in a mellow, red-brick building which was one of the first to be constructed after the Great Fire in 1694. The café offers excellent value for money and is popular with local people. You can sit inside, which is simply furnished, but generously supplied with books and magazines to browse through, or, weather permitting, you can sit in the lovely, enclosed garden, which is enlivened by the presence of a friendly cat and by the insistent cries of the peafowl in the grounds of the nearby castle. There is a good range of home-made lunch dishes, mostly, though not exclusively, vegetarian. Baked goods include tea loaf, flapjacks, scones and fruit cake, and there are puddings and ice creams too. Snacks such as sandwiches and ploughman's are always available, and drinks include tea, coffee, fruit tea, hot chocolate, Bovril, milk, squash, mineral water and fruit juice. Dogs are welcome in the garden, but must be "poop scooped if necessary". Smokers may light up in the garden if "in dire need".

Open: 10.00am-4.00pm Monday to Saturday, April to September; 10.00am-3.00pm Monday to Saturday, October to March. Closed Christmas and New Year. Telephone: 01926 407476/497732

The Walk

At the south-west end of the High Street, almost opposite the Quaker Community Centre, stands one of Warwick's finest buildings, Lord Leycester Hospital. It was originally owned by the Guild of St George, but was substantially rebuilt when it came into new owner-ship after Henry VIII dissolved the guilds. In 1571 Robert Dudley, Earl of Leicester, acquired the property and transformed it into a place of retirement for old soldiers, a purpose it still serves today. Adjoining the hospital is a chapel built over the West Gate in the 12th century.

Go through the West Gate then turn right on Bowling Green Street, which becomes Theatre Street and leads to Saltisford, where you turn left. Soon after passing under a railway bridge, join the tow-path of the Saltisford Canal Arm. This was originally part of the War-wick and Birmingham Canal (later incorporated in the Grand Union) and was restored from dereliction between 1982 and 1988 by the Saltisford Canal Trust. Six families now live permanently afloat here, so please respect their privacy as you pass by. They have made colourful gardens by the towpath and their cats and dogs live in ap-parent harmony with a contented population of ducks, geese and swans.

When the path comes to an end, go up to the main road and turn left over a bridge. Cross the road and descend steps to join the tow-path of the Grand Union Canal. Turn right under the bridge (51) to regain the same heading as before. After going under the next bridge (carrying the A46 Warwick bypass), you reach Hatton Bottom Lock before arriving at another road bridge. Pass underneath it then take a path which leads up to the road. Turn left, following the road to its junction with the A4177 Birmingham road. Cross to a bridleway al-most opposite, which is also the access road for Wedgnock Park Farm. After passing the farm the bridleway continues as a well-defined track, keeping close to field edges. All the farmland on your right was once deer park, created by one of the descendants of Henry de Newburgh, the first post-Conquest Earl of Warwick.

When the final field is reached, the hedge takes a turn to the left, but you keep straight on to reach the top of the field. The imposing but rather grim 19th-century buildings of Hatton Sanatorium are to your left and Turkey Farm straight ahead. Turn right on another bri-dleway. This follows a clearly defined course, eventually joining a surfaced bridleway just after passing Deer Park Wood. Turn right on the bridleway and head back towards Warwick. Once you have crossed the A46, continue to another road then turn right on to Wedgnock Lane, then second left on to Upper Cape Road to return to the town centre.

Northgate will return you to High Street, and also enable you to visit St Mary's Church, which is notable for the magnificent Beauchamp Chapel, built between 1443 and 1464 in accordance with the will of Richard Beauchamp, 13th Earl of Warwick, Governor of Normandy and a hero of the Hundred Years' War, who died in Rouen in 1439. His elaborate memorial is the centrepiece of the

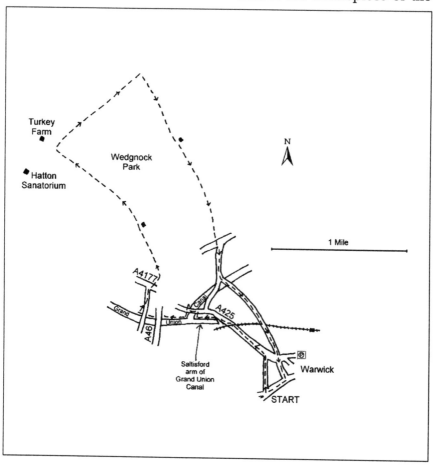

Quaker Community Café

chapel, which also contains memorials to Ambrose Dudley and Robert Dudley. Many people consider this to be the most beautiful chantry chapel in existence, a superb example of the Perpendicular style. Before the high altar is the tomb of Thomas Beauchamp, who commanded the English army at Crécy and died of the plague in 1369. Another high point – literally – of St Mary's is the view from the top of the tower. The steps seem endless but it really is worth the effort for a different perspective on Warwick.

𝒲𝒶𝓁𝓀 3: 𝒦𝑒𝓃𝒾𝓁𝓌𝑜𝓇𝓉𝒽

Start/finish: Castle Hill, Kenilworth; grid reference 280724.

Summary: An easy circular walk, using well-defined footpaths and bridleways through peaceful woods and fields. The charm of this countryside may come as a surprise to those who have only driven through modern Kenilworth.

Length: 6½ miles/10.5km.

Maps: OS Landranger 139 and 140, OS Pathfinder 955.

Buses/Coaches: Stagecoach Midland Red X16 and X18 Stratford to Coventry via Kenilworth, daily (the X18 stops on Castle Hill, by the tea shop); X14 Leamington to Warwick University via Kenilworth, Monday to Saturday; X17 Leamington to Coventry via Kenilworth, Monday to Saturday; 114 Leamington to Coventry via Kenilworth, Monday to Saturday; Travel West Midlands 12/112 Leamington to Coventry via Kenilworth, daily; A Line Travel 539 Coventry to Warwick via Kenilworth, Monday to Saturday; National Express 337 Brixham to Coventry via Kenilworth, daily; 460 Stratford to London via Kenilworth, daily.

Trains: Nearest stations are Warwick, Leamington and Coventry.

Parking: Public car parks at Borrowell Road and Abbey End in Kenilworth. The main car park by the castle is only for those visiting the castle, but there is another small parking area nearby.

The Tea Shop
Time For Tea, 40 Castle Hill, Kenilworth.

Fortunate in its situation on one of Kenilworth's finest streets, this is a lovely building, its mellow brick façade belonging to the 17th or 18th century but concealing an earlier, heavily beamed interior. The exterior is enhanced by the green and white paintwork; the sunny, south-facing interior by gingham curtains and a collection of teapots. Service is warm and friendly and this is a popular place with locals and tourists alike. There is a good range of home-made soups and hot lunches, all of which are suitable for vegetarians. Snacks include pitta pockets, baguettes, sandwiches and salads, and there's a special children's snack menu. Traditional temptations on offer include teacakes, muffins, crumpets, potato cakes, scones, pancakes,

Time for Tea in Kenilworth

and a variety of home-made cakes. There is the usual range of hot and cold drinks and also a number of speciality teas. Ice cream is available in summer, to eat in or take away. Time For Tea is a member of the Tea Council's Guild of Teashops.

Open: 10.30am-5.00pm Wednesday to Sunday. Closed Christmas week. Telephone: 01926 512675.

The Walk

Modern Kenilworth is an unremarkable town, but old Kenilworth is bursting with charm: Castle Hill, Castle Green, High Street and Abbey Fields are all as delightful as they are unexpected, and guarded by what English Heritage describes as "the finest and most extensive castle ruins in Britain". It's hard to argue with that when you see the magnificent red sandstone towers and keep glowing in the early morning or late afternoon sun.

Though there may have been an earlier wooden structure, the first stone castle at Kenilworth was built around 1120 by Henry I's Treasurer, Geoffrey de Clinton. In the 1150s a massive keep, which still survives, was added by de Clinton's son on the orders of Henry II, who later annexed the castle. It was greatly strengthened and ex-

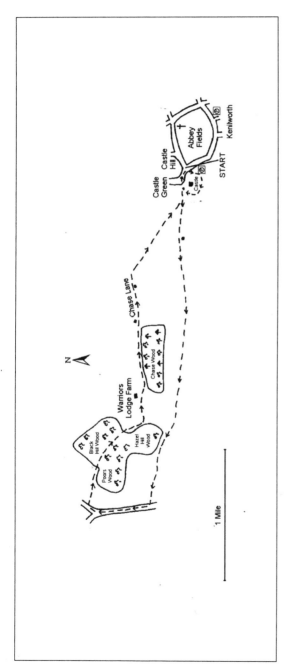

tended by both his son, King John, and his grandson, Henry III. The castle is linked with some of the most important names of English history:. men such as Henry V, who retired here after Agincourt; Edward II, who was imprisoned here before being taken to Berkeley, where he was murdered; and John of Gaunt, Duke of Lancaster and son of Edward III, who spent a fortune converting a bleak fortress into a luxurious palace. It was later enlarged and embellished still further by Robert Dudley, Earl of Leicester and favourite of Elizabeth I. Kenilworth's grandest moment came in 1575, when the Queen came for a lengthy visit and Dudley hosted a 19-day orgy of feasting and entertainment which would have bankrupted most of his contemporaries. After the Battle of Edgehill in 1642, the castle was partially demolished by Parliamentarian troops, and over the years it fell further into ruin, but still stands proud, gaunt and massive on its gentle slope. A footpath runs right round the castle – join it almost opposite Castle Hill and turn left, so that the castle is on your right. Start to walk round it, with rich, green pastureland soon coming into view on your left, where there was once a huge, artificial lake. In the early days this may have been defensive in purpose, a sort of extended moat, but it was later valued more for its aesthetic appeal, and in 1575 it enabled Dudley to stage a great water-borne pageant to entertain his royal visitor.

Walk round the castle and after passing a thatched cottage, turn left along a track, Purlieu Lane. Ignore all turnings and keep straight on to pass a farm. On entering a field, the path crosses substantial earthworks, all that remains of a hunting lodge named The Pleasance, which was built for Henry V on what was then the lakeside.

The path is waymarked and runs along field edges so there are no problems with route-finding. You'll soon see Chase Wood on your right, its name recalling the former hunting territory which went with Kenilworth Castle. Ignore any turnings until after you have left Chase Wood behind. Soon after this you'll cross a footbridge and find a choice of two paths. Turn right here, following a brook along the edge of Hazel Hill Wood. At the corner of the wood go straight on across fields, soon passing a small copse which has grown up around a group of ponds. Continue to Honiley Road and turn right.

Turn right again at a junction and shortly join a delightful bridleway, which soon enters woodland, with Black Hill Wood on the left, Poors Wood and Hazel Hill Wood on the right. At the far end of the woods the route remains obvious as you continue along field edges.

When you reach a farm track turn left, pass the buildings at Warriors Lodge Farm and turn right towards Chase Wood. Walk along its northern edge and then continue along Chase Lane. When a footpath crosses the lane, turn right to follow this well-trodden path diagonally across fields, with the final approach to Kenilworth offering marvellous views of the castle. Once back on Purlieu Lane turn left to explore Castle Green and return to Castle Hill.

Walk 4: Kenilworth to Warwick

Start: Abbey End, Kenilworth; grid reference 287720.

Finish: Old Square, Warwick; grid reference 280650.

Summary: An easy and enjoyable linear walk, making use of the Centenary Way to link the urban treasures of Kenilworth and Warwick by way of the attractive meadows and woods which lie between.

Length: 6 miles/9.6km.

Maps: OS Landrangers 140 and 151, OS Pathfinders 955 and 976.

Buses/Coaches: For details of all services to Warwick and Kenilworth see Walk 1 or 2 and Walk 3. Of these services, those which actually link the two towns are X16, X18 and 539 (also 337 and 460, but you'd be unlikely to use these National Express services for such a short, local journey).

Trains: There is currently no train service to Kenilworth. For details of trains to Warwick see Walk 1 or 2.

Parking: Public car parks in Warwick or Kenilworth.

The Tea Shop
The Bluebell, Abbey End, Kenilworth.

This is a pleasant place, with glass-topped pine tables, cane chairs and a cushioned sofa perhaps tempting fair-weather walkers to linger awhile on wet days. There's also plenty of less luxurious seating and a few chairs and tables outside. The menu is extensive, with plenty of hot lunch and snack dishes, including all-day breakfasts and other such favourites. Veggie breakfasts are available too, with a fair range of other vegetarian options. Traditional cream teas and other tea shop staples are on offer, and an excellent range of cakes. There are plenty of hot and cold drinks to choose from and there is an area for smokers. Dogs are welcome at the outside tables and will be provided with water. The Bluebell is popular with cyclists and walkers, especially for its takeaway menu.

Open: 8.00am-5.00pm Monday, Tuesday, Thursday, Friday, Saturday. 9.00am-5.00pm Sunday (3.30pm in winter). Telephone: 01926 857988.

Kenilworth Castle

The Walk

Abɔey End is the centre of modern Kenilworth, the focus having moved from the old High Street when the railway station (now closed) was opened in the 19th century. There's not a lot to detain you, other than The Bluebell, of course, so just walk to the top of Abbey End to find a large and very attractive park, Abbey Fields. Go more or less straight across to reach the red sandstone ruins of the abbey, founded in 1122. It was once one of the largest in the country but, following the Dissolution, much of its stone was used for repairs to the castle. Go through the abbey ruins then follow the path as it turns right to St Nicholas's Church at the end of a pollarded lime avenue. After admiring the superb Norman doorway, take a path leading up to High Street, the centre of medieval Kenilworth, with a rich variety of buildings spanning several centuries. Turn left along High Street, which runs into Castle Hill. The magnificent castle ruins are in front of you now (for details see Walk 3) as you descend to Castle Road. Cross over and look for a gate into the castle grounds opposite a pub, the Queen and Castle. Join the Centenary Way here, which takes you past the curtain wall then up a bank to the path which leads to the castle entrance. Turn left towards the car park and then right on a track as far as a sign for Grounds Farm, then left. Very soon, fork right, staying on the main track, to reach a gate by a

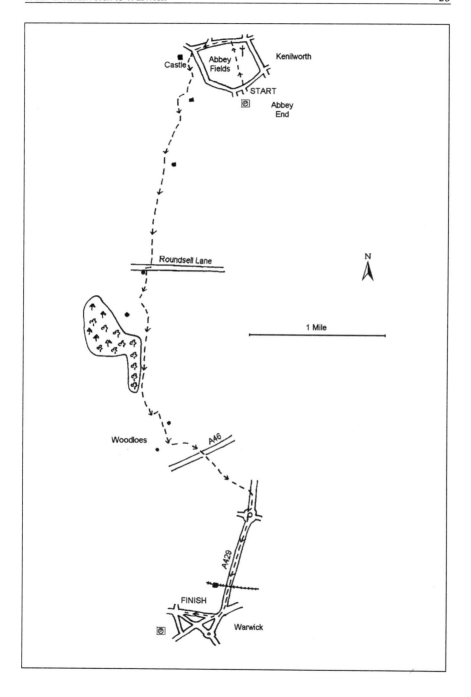

cattle grid. Go diagonally right towards another gate, where two signposts are visible.

Go through the gate and straight on along a bridleway. At the next cluster of waymarks turn left, still on the bridleway. Pass a pond and cross a large pasture towards a fence at the far side, where you turn right, passing a pond and crossing a footbridge. Go diagonally on a well-trodden path across the next field, through a bridle gate and forward to another footbridge. The route is unmistakable now, passing to the right of Oaks Farm, then through a gate and straight on along the edges of long, narrow fields, with a brook on your right, a hedge on your left.

On reaching Roundsell (or Rouncil) Lane, turn right for a short distance then cross to the entrance to Goodrest Farm. A concrete track leads to the farm across fields grazed by cattle, but before you reach the farm a stile on the left gives access to a footpath which veers slightly right away from the edge of a field to a stile below a big ash tree. A clear path runs ahead over rough pasture with a dense hedge on the left, full of sloes, haws and blackberries in October.

You'll soon reach a waymarked post which points through the trees to a stile on the left. Ignore this and take the path running to the right. The hedge should be on your left, and you'll notice a distinct dyke on your right. The path cuts across the end of it. You soon come to a path over a golf course on the left – ignore this. Stay on the Centenary Way, shortly going over another stile and continuing along the edge of the next field, ignoring another footpath on the left.

The path now leads through woodland of hazel, ash and field maple, and this is a very attractive part of the walk, despite the roar of the A46 ahead. Leaving the wood, the path takes you onto the edge of the golf course. Over to your left is Blacklow Hill, where Piers Gaveston, the lover of Edward II, was beheaded in 1312 at the behest of the Earl of Warwick and other discontented barons jealous of his power and influence.

Keep to the right-hand edge of the field and you can now see the tower of Warwick's beautiful St Mary's Church ahead. At the far end of the field the path bends left, still following the hedge. Ahead is an old, stone house, Woodlands Farm. Continue to a stile in the corner, climb over, cross a footbridge and go straight ahead over a field. At a junction keep on in the same direction, ignoring a left turn. Pass Woodloes Farm and go forward to a surfaced track, where you turn left to the main road. Turn right into Warwick, still on the Centenary Way.

Walk 5: Royal Leamington Spa

Start/finish: Royal Leamington Spa Station, grid reference 315653.

Summary: This enjoyable circular walk on well-defined footpaths indicates just how easy it is to escape the town for the country. It includes a stretch of the Grand Union Canal and a site of some historical significance at Offchurch.

Length: 6 miles/9.6km.

Maps: OS Landranger 151, OS Pathfinder 976.

Buses/Coaches: Stagecoach Midland Red X16 and X18 Stratford to Coventry via Leamington, daily; X12 and X14 Warwick University to Leamington, daily except Sundays during university vacations; X17 Coventry to Leamington, Monday to Saturday; 114 Kenilworth and/or Coventry to Leamington, Monday to Saturday; 19/19A Stratford and/or Hampton Magna to Bishops Tachbrook via Leamington, Monday to Saturday; 61 Lowsonford to Leamington, Wednesdays and Saturdays; 63/64/65 Rugby and/or Napton to Leamington, Monday to Saturday; 66 Warwick to Leamington, every few minutes Monday to Saturday; 68 Cubbington to Leamington, Monday to Saturday; 274 Stratford to Leamington, Monday to Saturday; Travel West Midlands 12/12A/112 Coventry to Leamington, daily; A Line Travel 538 Coventry to Leamington, Monday to Saturday; Village Bus (A&M Cars) Harbury to Leamington, Wednesdays and Fridays, and Bishops Itchington to Leamington, Tuesdays and Thursdays; Cambridge Coach Services 71 Bromsgrove and/or Worcester to Cambridge via Leamington, daily; National Express 310 Bradford to Portsmouth/Poole via Leamington, daily; 337 Brixham to Coventry via Leamington, daily; 460 Stratford to London via Leamington, daily; 480 Kidderminster to London via Leamington, daily; 728 Inverness to Oxford via Leamington, daily.

Trains: Central Trains Stratford to Leamington and Worcester to Leamington, daily; Chiltern Railways Birmingham to London via Leamington, daily; Thames Trains London to Stratford via Leamington, daily; Virgin Cross Country Glasgow/Edinburgh to London – Bournemouth – Brighton via Leamington, daily.

Parking: Public car parks in Leamington.

The Tea Shop
Pulse, 19B High Street, Leamington.

Though not in the most salubrious part of town, Pulse is clean and pleasant inside, with pine furnishings and cheerful decor enhanced

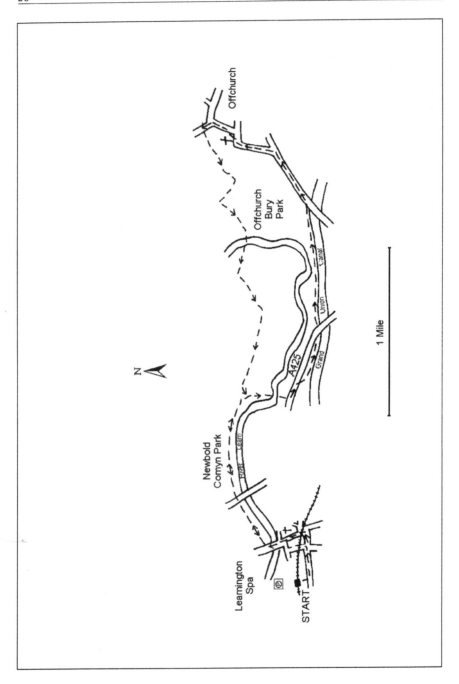

by plants. There are papers and magazines to read, while friendly staff serve up the cheapest drinks and meals in Leamington. Even that new fashion essential, the cappuccino, is cheap here. Other types of coffee are available, as well as teas (including fruit, herbal and decaffeinated), hot chocolate, soft drinks, milk and spring water. The menu is vegetarian (some meals are also suitable for vegans), and snacks include sandwiches, baguettes, croissants, ciabatta, and rolls with imaginative fillings such as brie with apple, grape, cranberry, avocado or kiwi. If you want a hot meal you can choose from stir-fry, curry, thali, pasta, chilli, all-day breakfasts and many more. There is also a range of cakes, pastries and other baked goods. Baby changing facilities and baby bottle warming are available, guide dogs are welcome and smoking is permitted. Pulse is staffed by volunteers working for the charity Mind (Mid-Warwickshire) as part of a community project.

Open: 10.30am-5.00pm Monday to Friday. Telephone: 01926 450745.

The Walk

Leaving the rail station, turn left on to High Street, pass under a railway bridge and there is Pulse in front of you on the corner of High Street and Bath Street. Go left on Bath Street to the town centre, which is based around The Parade, just the other side of the River Leam. After crossing the river you will see the Royal Pump Room on your left and Jephson Gardens on your right.

The saline springs which were to make Leamington's fortune were first commercially exploited in the 1780s, when the present town was a small village. Close to the church there rose a spring of saline water, its health-giving properties known locally for centuries and freely available to all villagers. Realising its commercial potential, two local men, Benjamin Satchwell and William Abbots, began to search for a second spring and found one in 1784, on land in what is now Bath Street (number 34). This land belonged to Abbots himself, and soon baths and a hotel were built and Leamington's rise to fame had begun. By 1835 most of the present town centre had been laid out. In 1838 the charismatic Dr Henry Jephson, who had opened the Pump Room in 1814, secured royal authority to add "Royal" and "Spa" to the name of the now fashionable town. Leamington's status grew rapidly as the wealthy came to "take the waters", which were thought to be a cure for every conceivable ailment. You can still sample the waters at the Pump Room, and still admire the elegant Regency terraces, squares and crescents which abound, many of them painted white and with fine detail in the form of fretted ironwork verandas and superb doorways. Though the spa cult has faded, today's colourful, cosmopolitan Leamington still flourishes, its vitality and style owing much to its large Asian and student populations.

The large and beautifully landscaped Jephson Gardens pay tribute to the man who first put Leamington firmly on the map. Flower beds blaze with colour for much of the year, but the gardens also provide cool, shady oases of green, thanks to mature trees and the soothing presence of the River Leam.

Walk through Jephson Gardens to the far side, cross Willes Road and go straight on, choosing one of a network of paths which threads through a wooded nature reserve beside the River Leam. On reaching Newbold Comyn Park, walk uphill by a leisure centre until another path is revealed on the right. This takes you through more woodland and grassland close to the river, until eventually a footbridge leads across the river, where the waymarks indicate that you have joined the Centenary Way, albeit briefly.

Pass through a car park to Radford Road, turn left, cross and look for an access point to the towpath of the Grand Union Canal. Follow

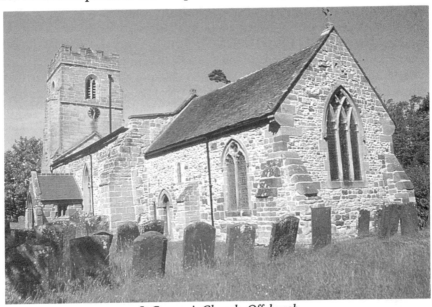

St Gregory's Church, Offchurch

it to the left, past Radford Semele to Radford Bottom Lock, where you join a road and turn right, passing Bury Lodge then crossing with care to a footway. At the next junction turn left to Offchurch, a village of brick and thatch with pleasant views over the valley of the meandering Leam. The village boasts a possible connection with Offa, the most notable ruler (from 757 to 796) of the Saxon kingdom Mercia. St Gregory's Church is said to have been built by Offa in memory of his son Fremund, who was murdered nearby. It was re-built in the 11th century and little of the original Saxon church re-mains. However, in 1833, during restoration work, two pieces of curiously carved red sandstone were found, which were thought to be part of the lid of a stone coffin, possibly Offa's. They were later built into the north wall of the nave.

Offa is also said to have built a fort or palace on or near to the site now occupied by the 19th-century house Offchurch Bury. Skeletons have been dug up at the Bury (the name comes from the Saxon word for fortified dwelling) on at least two occasions. Excavations in 1866 also revealed a Saxon burial ground near the church, with weapons and jewellery dating back to 650.

The churchyard is being managed as part of the Living Church-yard Scheme to encourage wildlife. Local volunteers have created a summer meadow, laid the perimeter hedges in the traditional way, planted woodland and installed nest boxes and bat boxes.

Walk through the churchyard and turn left (towards Hunningham and Cubbington) then left again at a T-junction. Go past Corner Cot-tage then into a field grazed by horses. Turn left on a well-trodden path and over a stile to the next field. A clear path now takes you across Offchurch Bury Park. After crossing a bridge, turn left by a ce-dar tree and follow a hedge to the end of the field then turn right to a footbridge over the Leam. A few paces further on fork left to enter an-other field. Turn right by the river then veer away from it, towards the left. A stile leads to the next field and you go straight on by the right-hand hedge to a gap, where you join a path diagonally across another field.

Go through a gap to join another path and turn left past a strip of woodland bordering a golf course. At a junction turn right, and near the far side of the field turn right on a path by a Local Nature Reserve sign. As you approach the club house, bear left to go through a car park to Newbold Comyn Leisure Centre. Retrace your steps into Leamington.

Walk 6: Hatton

Start/finish: Hatton Station, grid reference 224664.

Summary: This effortless circular walk through very pleasant countryside takes you along the Grand Union Canal's famous Hatton Flight, known to many as the Stairway to Heaven. The walk also provides the opportunity to visit Hatton Country World, where the tea room is just one of many attractions available.

Length: 6 miles/9.6km.

Maps: OS Landranger 151, OS Pathfinder 976.

Buses/Coaches: Stagecoach Midland Red 19/19A Stratford to Bishops Tachbrook, Monday to Saturday – get off at Hampton Magna.

Trains: Central Trains Stratford to Leamington and Worcester to Leamington via Hatton, daily; Chiltern Railways London to Birmingham via Hatton, daily (change at Warwick or Leamington on Sundays); Thames Trains London to Stratford via Hatton, daily (change at Warwick or Leamington on Sundays).

Parking: At Hatton Station, Hatton Locks or Hatton Country World.

The Tea Shop

The Greedy Pig, Hatton Country World, Dark Lane, Hatton.

Hatton Country World is home to a variety of attractions, many of them housed in a collection of 19th-century farm buildings. Apart from the UK's largest craft centre, there is also a shopping village, an antiques centre, a plant centre and a farm park with 40 traditional and rare breeds of cattle, sheep, goats, pigs and poultry. The farm park also features farming demonstrations, sheepdog displays, falconry, pony rides and lots of small animals to feed and stroke. With all this going on, it follows that the Greedy Pig is less a tea room, more a busy family café (there is also a quieter restaurant/bar) and might be best visited mid-week, out of season. A soft play centre (or bouncy barn) for children adjoins the café, and a large window enables you to keep an eye on your children while you indulge in traditional favourites such as scones, fruit cake, cherry cake or sandwiches. There is a good choice of hot meals and snacks, and the usual range of drinks. Smoking is permitted, a baby changing room is provided and there's an outdoor patio. Dogs are welcome, on a lead, but may not be taken into the farm park. An admission charge applies to the farm park and bouncy barn, but not to the café or shops.

Open: 9.30am-6.30pm daily (7.30pm summer weekends and school summer holidays). Telephone: 01926 843411.

The Grand Union Canal, near Hatton Station

The Walk

Leave Hatton Station and join the towpath of the Grand Union Canal, heading east towards Warwick. When you reach John's Bridge (55) go up to Dark Lane and turn right, soon joining a permissive path which takes you to Hatton Country World. You'll find the Greedy Pig near the farm park ticket office.

Having visited the café, return to the lane and turn left. Shortly after passing a pair of farm cottages the lane bends to the right. Join a footpath on the left here, walking along the right-hand edges of two fields. In a third field go diagonally towards the far corner then through a gate and on to a farm drive. Turn left, passing through a pleasant pastoral landscape grazed by cattle.

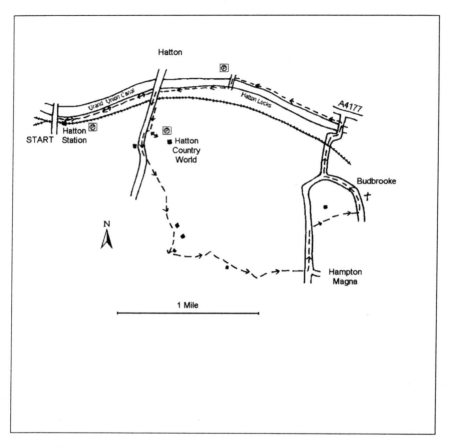

Reaching Wilderness Cottage turn left, with rolling fields and woodland on your right and the walled garden of Grove Farm on your left. Ignore a branching footpath on the right. Before long Warwick comes into view ahead, and soon after this you pass Park Lodge and Grove Park House.

A little further on, join a footpath on the left which runs along a field edge. At the corner go through a gap and continue in the same direction but now on the other side of the hedge. Reaching the road at Hampton Magna, turn left. This pleasant, leafy lane is bordered by a strip of woodland on the right, and open fields on the left. After the woodland comes to an end, join a footpath on the right. Follow the left-hand field edge to a footbridge, cross over and turn right to continue in the same direction, with a farm on your left. After passing the farm, cross a stile and bear left across a field, aiming for a detached brick house some distance to the right of the church at Budbrooke. A stile gives on to the farm drive, where you turn right, then left at the road.

Walk through Budbrooke, passing St Michael's Church, which has Norman origins though it has been largely rebuilt. At a road junction turn right towards the canal and Hatton. After crossing Ugly Bridge (this concrete horror could hardly be more appropriately named), take a path on the left which leads to the towpath. Walk towards Hatton (i.e. with the canal on your left). After passing bridge 53 you're at the most dramatic section of the Hatton Flight, a two-mile stretch of 21 locks which lifts the canal out of the Avon Valley. It's the most impressive part of a modernising programme undertaken on the Grand Union in the 1930s in an attempt to compete with the Great Western Railway. The remains of the old narrow locks are visible beside the newer wide ones. Sadly, financial constraints meant the programme was never completed. The canal played a vital role in carrying raw materials during the Second World War, but trade declined soon afterwards and was finally killed off by the motorways. Today, however, the canal is busy with leisure craft and its towpath is popular with walkers.

At bridge 54 the towpath changes sides and a retrospective glance here will reveal a fine view down to Warwick, dominated by the tower of St Mary's Church. It is thought the church was used to align the locks when they were first constructed in the 1790s.

Carry on along the towpath, passing a former stables now converted into a useful shop selling maps, books, gifts and refreshments. When you come to bridge 55, stay on the towpath if you're returning to Hatton Station or go up to Dark Lane if you started the walk at Hatton Country World.

Walk 7: Stratford and Welcombe Hills

Start/finish: Waterside, Stratford-upon-Avon; grid reference 204548.

Summary: A short and very easy circular walk to a fine viewpoint in an enjoyable country park on the edge of Stratford – ideal for a relaxing evening after a day spent sightseeing, or just to gain relief from all things Shakespearean.

Length: 4 miles/6.4km.

Maps: OS Landranger 151, OS Pathfinders 997 and 998.

Buses/Coaches: Stagecoach Midland Red X16 and X18 Coventry to Stratford, daily; X50 Birmingham to Oxford via Stratford, daily; 19 Bishops Tachbrook to Stratford, Monday to Saturday; 21 Bourton-on-the-Water to Stratford, daily; 22 Broadway to Stratford, Monday to Saturday; 23 Brailes to Stratford, Monday to Saturday; 24 Bearley to Stratford, Monday to Saturday; 25/26 Redditch to Stratford, Monday to Saturday; 27 Pebworth to Stratford, Monday to Saturday; 28 Evesham to Stratford, Monday to Saturday; 270 Banbury to Stratford, Monday to Saturday; 274 Leamington to Stratford, Monday to Saturday; Barry's Coaches Moreton to Stratford, Wednesdays and Fridays; Cambridge Coach Services 71 Bromsgrove and/or Worcester to Cambridge via Stratford, daily; National Express 337 Brixham to Coventry via Stratford, daily; 339 Birmingham to Bristol via Stratford, daily; 460 London to Stratford, daily; 480 Birmingham to London via Stratford, daily.

Trains: Central Trains Leamington to Stratford and Worcester to Stratford, daily; Thames Trains London to Stratford, daily.

Parking: Public car parks in Stratford.

The Tea Shop

Bruno's Bakery, 30 Greenhill Street, Stratford.

If you arrive in Stratford by train and walk towards the town centre, you'll reach Bruno's within a couple of minutes. If you're trying to find it from the town centre, just walk up Wood Street to the market place then go forward on to Greenhill Street. A tiny place, with just four tables, the tea room is tacked onto a bread shop, and might seem an unlikely choice in a town bursting at the seams with both traditional and trendy upmarket tea rooms. But not all of those welcome walkers, not all of them offer good value and some of them are so busy that getting a table is out of the question at peak times, unless you're prepared to queue. Bruno's is tucked away out of sight of most tourists so it's often quiet, and in terms of value for money and friendliness of welcome there's nowhere in Stratford to compare. The menu is fairly limited, although you can choose from snacks such as sandwiches and soups as well as from a full range of baked goods – everything that's on sale in the shop, in fact. All portions are substantial and a fair range of drinks is available. Vegetarians should ask for details of suitability as some items may contain lard.

Open: 9.00am-5.00pm Monday to Saturday. Telephone: 01789 293732.

The River Avon at Stratford

The Walk

William Shakespeare was born in Stratford in 1564, and died there in 1616. His birthplace soon became a place of literary pilgrimage, but it was not until 1769 that the phenomenon which is Stratford tourism really began, when the town first staged a festival in honour of its most famous son. This proved to be the catalyst which transformed an attractive but unremarkable small town into a tourist honeypot second only to London. Stratford makes the most of the connection, and top of the list for most visitors are the Shakespeare properties, five picturesque Tudor houses with Shakespeare family connections.

But you don't have to be a Shakespeare fan to enjoy Stratford, which has been a market town since 1169. In a way, this is still what it does best – see it on a Friday, when the blue and white awnings go up over the stalls at the top of Wood Street, and local people flock in from the outlying villages. And wander round the town centre, which still maintains its medieval grid pattern – many fine old buildings survive from Tudor times and even earlier, and there are also elegant Georgian buildings, evidence of continuing prosperity.

Stratford's charms are further enhanced by the presence of the River Avon and the Stratford Canal, and there are pleasant walks beside both. The canal basin is usually crammed with colourful narrowboats, and the surrounding gardens attract lively, cosmopolitan crowds, as well as jugglers, mime artists and other performers.

From Waterside, walk up Bridge Street to the five-ways junction at the heart of town, then go along Henley Street, where there are usually long queues for Shakespeare's Birthplace. Turn left at the main road, cross at the lights and walk along Clopton Road. Ignore all turnings, eventually crossing a cattle grid and continuing to a junction. Turn right, following a leafy avenue to Clopton Tower, a folly built in the 1850s in the grounds of Clopton House.

Turn left on the Monarch's Way to enter Welcombe Hills Country Park and keep straight on. Welcombe Hills comprises a large area of open land promoted as a relic of Shakespeare's pastoral countryside. He probably walked over the hills frequently as he had family connections in Snitterfield, just to the north. The hills are surprisingly rich in wildlife and you can expect to see and hear a variety of birds. There is open access on foot through much of the area, so the walk described here may be varied at will.

The path climbs gently, and as the ground levels out an obelisk comes into view on the right. When you come to a fenced woodland, Top Spinney, pass to the left of it on a footpath, leaving the Monarch's Way. At the far end of the wood turn right towards the obelisk. Welcombe Hotel now comes into view, a red-brick mansion with multiple chimneys. It was originally a private house built in 1866, replacing an earlier one on the same site. It became a hotel in 1931.

Walk to the obelisk on Monument Hill, which was erected as a memorial to Mark Philips, MP and philanthropist, who was born in Lancashire in 1800, and died at Welcombe in 1873. There are superb views from the foot of the obelisk, including the Cotswolds and the hills at Burton Dassett.

Descend from the obelisk to a path which leads to the hotel. Don't go towards the hotel but look for a stile which gives access to Green Hill. When you come to the corner of a walled kitchen garden, turn left and follow a well-trodden path across the hillside. The area is dotted with hawthorn trees, which attract fieldfares and redwings in autumn. The path descends and continues past the hotel, through limestone grassland which supports many wild flowers. After descending Green Hill the path then rises gently to pass Bluecap Covert, probably named after the blue tit, for which bluecap is a local name.

Go through a kissing gate into South Field and straight across to another gate into a large pasture. Go diagonally left to the hedge and continue beside it, eventually emerging onto Welcombe Road. Walk towards Stratford. At the main road turn right then shortly left, passing two car parks and a leisure centre before the road (Bridgeway) swings round to the Tourist Information Centre and Bridgefoot. Turn right for Waterside, Bridge Street and the town centre.

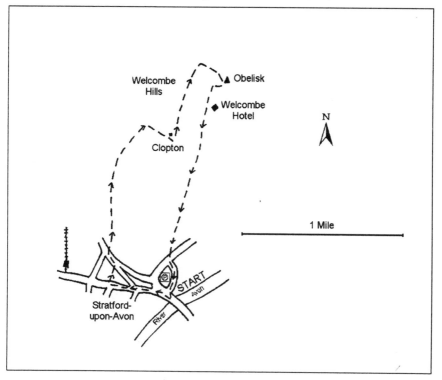

Walk 8: Stratford and the Stour Valley

Start: Alderminster, grid reference 230487.

Finish: Stratford-upon-Avon, grid reference 204550.

Summary: An enjoyable linear walk through the pleasant, pastoral countryside of the Stour Valley, visiting Preston-on-Stour, probably Warwickshire's most peaceful and unspoilt village. Though it's an easy walk, some of the footpaths are poorly maintained and you may have to clamber over a couple of fences. The River Stour is affected by toxic blue-green algae so keep dogs out of it.

Length: 6 miles/9.6km.

Maps: OS Landranger 151, OS Pathfinders 997, 998 and 1021.

Buses/Coaches: For details of buses to Stratford see Walk 7. To do this linear walk use Stagecoach Midland Red X50 Birmingham to Oxford services, which operate daily (and hourly) via Alderminster. Or use the 23, Stratford to Brailes via Alderminster, Monday to Saturday. This one also calls at Preston-on-Stour, allowing you to start the walk there if you would prefer to shorten it a little.

Trains: For details of trains to Stratford see Walk 7. There is no train service to Alderminster.

Parking: Public car parks in Stratford.

The Tea Shop

The Shire Horse Restaurant, Shire Horse Centre, Clifford Road, Stratford.

Though shire horses are obviously the main attraction here, there are also rare breeds of sheep, goats, cattle, pigs and poultry, along with an owl sanctuary, falconry displays and various activities for children. The restaurant is housed in a converted threshing barn with exposed roof timbers and brick walls hung with banners, shields, Shakespearean scenes and old monochrome photos of horse-drawn wagons and caravans. It's a spacious place with plenty of seating, not only inside, but also in a pleasant garden area, and there is a play barn for young children. Dogs may be left in the courtyard or reception area. The menu is extensive, with plenty of cooked meals to choose from, as well as a range of snacks. Daily specials are chalked up on a blackboard, and there are always vegetarian options. Baked goods include scones and a variety of cakes, while puddings and ice cream are also available. The usual range of hot and cold drinks is complemented by fruit and flower wines such as sloe, elderberry, cowslip, orange and peach. There are both smoking and non-smoking areas.

Open: 10.00am-5.00pm daily except winter Thursdays and Fridays. Telephone: 01789 266276.

Representatives from the Shire Horse Centre

The Walk

Begin by taking the bus from Stratford to Alderminster. Though there's little of interest in this village, the church is worth a look. It's of Norman origin but was extensively restored in the 19th century, and it stands in a fine, leafy churchyard graced by horse chestnut trees laden with conkers each autumn.

Walk back beside the road towards Stratford, passing several pairs of estate houses with Gothic windows. After you pass the last of them, continue for a short distance to find a stile rather concealed by trees on your left. Climb over to stand at the top of a bank overlooking the wide, flat expanse of the Stour Valley.

Turn right, parallel with the road, along the top of the bank, soon passing through hawthorn woodland before climbing a stile and bearing left towards a farm. A footbridge spans a tributary, and then an obvious route suggests itself along the bottom of a bank. Approaching the farmhouse, turn right to a waymarked gate. The path passes to the right of former farm buildings, now converted into homes, and is adequately waymarked. Continue to Wimpstone Lane and turn left.

Having crossed the River Stour, continue a few paces to a bend in the lane, then join a footpath on the right. Follow a hedge to its end by a pumping station and turn left beside a fence and a gappy line of hawthorns. As you approach the end of the field, veer a little right to a footbridge. Go straight on across an arable field, the river on your right. As the river moves away, keep straight on towards another sewage works. Once past this keep going in the same direction, roughly parallel with a concrete track, across open pasture towards a large oak tree close to a road junction. A gate left of the oak gives access to Preston Lane. Turn right.

As you approach the river again turn left towards a farm, The Gables, then left on a footpath enclosed between hedges. Ahead is Preston, with a cluster of roofs crowding the church and, on the left, a timber-framed manor house. The path reaches a lane and continues opposite to the village. However, it's more rewarding to go to the right, passing more interesting houses which line the lane as it swings round to the village centre. There are some lovely houses here, and the church is worth a visit. Dedicated to St Mary, it lies at the top of a yew avenue above a green. Built of warm, glowing stone, its medieval fabric was remodelled in the Gothic style between 1753 and 1757, for James West of Alscot Park. Sadly, this early example of 18th-century Gothic Revival has been damaged by 19th- and 20th-century alterations and additions.

Take the lane which goes to the left of the village green, passing more cottages. To the left is a gated road to Atherstone, but we turn right, past Park Farm. More lovely houses line this narrow lane as it takes you to a T-junction where you turn left, passing The Old Vicarage.

Go straight ahead through a copse then across grassland. Over to your right, across the river, is a large, fortified mansion, Alscot Park. This, like the church, is an example of the early Gothic Revival style

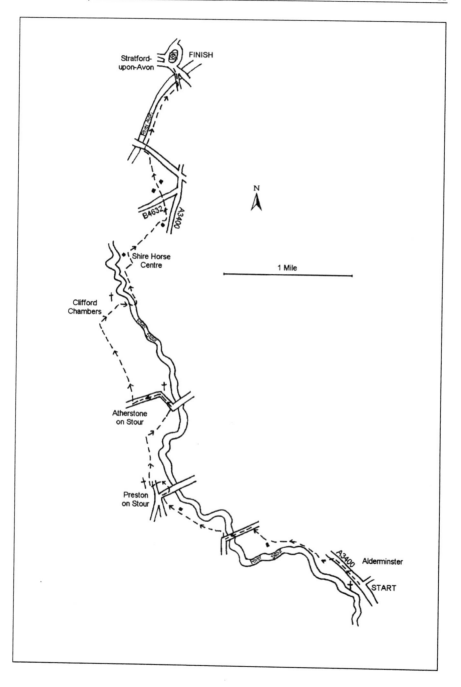

and was built for the same man, James West, Joint Secretary to the Treasury. It stands in attractive, wooded parkland.

Pass to the left of a tumulus (prehistoric burial mound) and through a gate just to the left of a plantation. The path follows the edge of the plantation to a junction with another path, where you turn right. When the path joins a lane, turn left into Atherstone on Stour, where there is little to detain you. Walk on along the lane until, some 300 metres from the village, you can join a footpath on the right.

When you reach a T-junction turn right towards Clifford Chambers. A lime avenue leads to the centre, where attractive houses of stone, brick and timber line a grass-bordered, tree-shaded street. There is an interesting church of Norman origin, with a Perpendicular tower, and nearby stands a 17th-century manor rebuilt by Sir Edwin Lutyens in the 1920s. The path goes past here and bears right to The Old Mill. It then takes you across the millrace and turns right before crossing the River Stour.

Once across the river, turn left, the way now clearly marked across meadows grazed by cattle, sheep and shire horses. The river, bordered by willows, is patrolled by herons, while dwarf cattle, goats and fancy poultry may be seen as you approach the Shire Horse Centre.

The shire horses' ancestors carried medieval knights into battle, undeterred by the 30 stone (190kg) weight of a man in full armour. The horses themselves weigh about a ton, stand taller than most men at the shoulder and are the gentlest of gentle giants. There are 20 at the centre and they can be seen engaged in their traditional work of ploughing and harvesting, though they are also used to haul wagonloads of visitors.

Pass the livery stables then turn left, past barns, to the main entrance and the restaurant. An entrance fee is payable if you wish to go into the Shire Horse Centre, but this does not apply to the restaurant.

Leaving the restaurant, go straight ahead, with the car park on your left, across a field towards a farm. After passing some brick barns the path turns right, then left along the field edge but only for about 25 metres, until you can join a path running diagonally across the field.

Cross Clifford Lane to a footpath almost opposite, next to the entrance to Cross O'th'Hill Farm. Walk diagonally across a field to the far right corner. Go over a stile and forward to a track, turn right and then join a footpath running immediately to the right of a barbed wire fence. Take care, as the path may be overgrown, concealing rough and uneven ground. Head directly towards the spire of Holy Trinity Church at Stratford. After going through a gate, walk down a bank to join a surfaced path and continue towards town. Turn left below Seven Meadows Road (built on the course of the former Stratford and Midland Railway) to the River Avon. Turn right under the road to find a footbridge, giving you a choice as to which bank of the river you follow into Stratford.

Walk 9: Shottery and Wilmcote

Start: Anne Hathaway's Cottage, Shottery; grid reference 185547.

Finish: Mary Arden's House, Wilmcote; grid reference 164582.

Summary: A very easy linear walk linking two popular and picturesque Shakespearean properties. It makes use of the towpath of the Stratford Canal, and the terrain is level throughout, with only one stile. Expect large crowds at the two houses at peak periods. Anne Hathaway's Cottage is just over a mile from the centre of Stratford – follow the signs if you want to walk from town.

Length: 3 miles/5km.

Maps: OS Landranger 151, OS Pathfinder 997.

Buses/Coaches: Stagecoach Midland Red 1/2 Stratford Town Minibus and Stratford Blue Shuttle from Bridge Street and Wood Street to Anne Hathaway's Cottage, every few minutes, Monday to Saturday; 25 Redditch to Stratford via Wilmcote, Monday to Saturday; Johnsons Henley to Redditch via Shottery, Thursdays; Guide Friday tour buses also serve both Shottery and Wilmcote, daily. For full details of services to Stratford see Walk 7.

Trains: Central Trains Leamington to Stratford and Worcester to Stratford via Wilmcote, daily; Thames Trains London to Stratford via Wilmcote, daily – but Thames don't stop at Wilmcote on Sundays. Anne Hathaway's Cottage is less than a mile from Stratford Station.

Parking: Public car parks in Stratford, or at Shottery (Anne Hathaway's Cottage or the Cottage Tea Garden).

The Tea Shop

The Cottage Tea Garden, Cottage Lane, Shottery, Stratford.

Just across the lane from Anne Hathaway's Cottage, this conservatory-style building is set in pleasant gardens by Shottery Brook. There is both inside and outside seating, and a friendly black cat is often in attendance. You can choose from a range of hot lunches, including jackets, Cornish pasties, curry and chilli con carne, as well as the usual scones, tea cakes, sandwiches, baguettes etc. Also available are ice creams, salads and a range of "Cotswold country lunches". Some choices are suitable for vegetarians. There is the usual range of hot and cold drinks. Guide dogs are welcome, and smokers may indulge in the garden, but not in the conservatory.

Open: 10.00am-5.00pm April to October. Telephone: 01789 293122.

Narrowboat on the Stratford Canal

The Walk

The former village of Shottery has now been swallowed up by Stratford, but still retains a little character of its own. It is famous for Anne Hathaway's Cottage, a picturesque, timber-framed and thatched farmhouse which was Anne's home until she married Shakespeare in 1582. It's set in a traditional English garden with an orchard, and close to a modest but lovely terrace of old, brick cottages not even noticed by many visitors.

The Shakespeare Birthplace Trust owns much of the property in and around Shottery village, and purchased the cottage in 1892, up to which time it had remained in Anne's family. The interior is furnished as it would have been in her day, mostly with pieces which actually belonged to the Hathaway family. A little further down the lane is the Shakespeare Tree Garden, also maintained by the Birthplace Trust, containing trees, shrubs and other plants mentioned by Shakespeare. It's open to the public at the same times as Anne Hathaway's Cottage. Dogs are not allowed.

Having explored Shottery, walk on along Cottage Lane until you see a footpath on the right. Follow it past several thatched cottages to reach Church Lane and turn left to the main road. Cross to a footpath almost opposite, signposted to Wilmcote.

A passageway between houses leads to Shottery Brook, which has a footpath on each bank. Take your pick and just follow the brook to the canal, where you turn left on a footpath. Construction began on the Stratford Canal in 1793 but it was 1816 before it was completed, though it ran for only 25 miles between King's Norton and Stratford. It prospered for a time, but soon began to suffer from competition, and in 1856 the canal company sold out to the Great Western Railway. Decline and decay followed, but in the 1960s the southern section was restored by the National Trust, which later handed it over to British Waterways, which was better able to maintain it.

At bridge 63, cross the canal to the towpath but continue in the same direction, quite soon reaching the first locks of the Wilmcote Flight, which is divided into three distinct parts: two outer groups of three and a central five. Eventually, having passed all the locks, you'll reach an ugly, concrete road bridge at Wilmcote Wharf; pass under it then go up to the road.

The railway station is just to your left. However, a right turn will bring you to Mary Arden's House, which you will surely want to visit before leaving Wilmcote. The village itself is a former quarrying centre with a Victorian church, two pubs and a shop. It offers little of interest to the visitor other than the beautiful Tudor farmhouse believed to be the home of Shakespeare's mother, Mary Arden, before she married John Shakespeare.

Mary Arden's House now forms part of the Shakespeare Countryside Museum, which comprises a wide range of displays and attractions. The farmhouse itself is furnished much as it would have been when Mary lived in it. There are actually two historic farms on the museum site, and the other farmhouse has a Victorian interior. In the nearby barns are displays of farm implements and other reminders of how life once was in the countryside. Also on site are a blacksmith's forge, a duck pond, a café and gift shop. There are picnic and play areas, too. In the fields are rare breeds of poultry, longhorn cattle and Cotswold sheep. There is also a falconry centre, with birds on display throughout the year and flying demonstrations daily.

Even if you don't intend to visit the museum, it's still well worth viewing the exterior of Mary Arden's House from the road. You may then retrace your steps to the railway station or wait on the tiny village green for a bus.

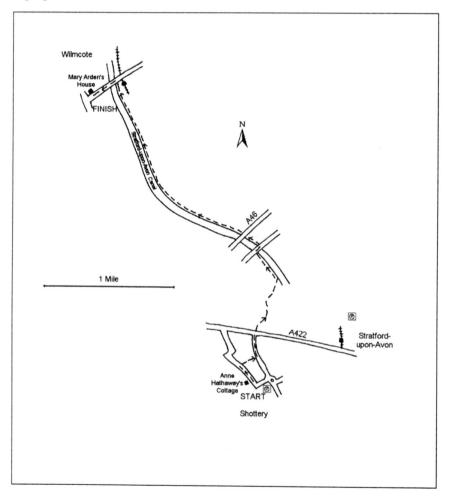

Walk 10: Charlecote

Start/finish: Charlecote Park, grid reference 263564.

Summary: An effortless circular walk which offers lovely views from Copdock Hill and
the chance to visit one of the finest houses in the Midlands, together with
its surrounding deer park. Please note that dogs are not allowed in Charlecote Park.

Length: 4 miles/6.4km.

Maps: OS Landranger 151, OS Pathfinder 998.

Buses/Coaches: Stagecoach Midland Red 18/X18 Stratford to Coventry via Charlecote,
daily; 274 Stratford to Leamington via Charlecote, Monday to Saturday.

Trains: Nearest station is Stratford.

Parking: National Trust car park opposite the main entrance to Charlecote Park,
intended for visitors to Charlecote. If you wish to leave your car here
while you go for a walk you may do so on weekdays, but not at
weekends. However, there are some parking places alongside the
road nearby.

The Tea Shop

The Orangery Restaurant, Charlecote Park, near Warwick.

The Orangery, an elegant stone building, is on your right as you approach the house. There are green-painted iron tables and chairs
outside and plenty of room inside too, where the walls are painted a
warm and welcoming deep pink and the atmosphere is pleasant and
relaxing. Be sure to sit outside, however, if you would appreciate the
colourful presence of the resident peafowl while you eat. The menu
includes a variety of hot lunch dishes, as well as old favourites such
as jackets, ploughman's, baguettes, soups and puddings. Afternoon
tea comes in traditional guise, with several set menus to choose
from, and cakes include flapjack, cherry slice, almond slice and
shortbread, some of which are suitable for vegetarians.

Open: 11.00am-5.30pm Friday to Tuesday, April to end of October. Telephone: 01789 470448.

Note: Charlecote Park is a National Trust property so an entrance fee is payable, except by Trust members, even if you intend only to visit the tea room. When the park is closed, or for those who don't wish to pay the entrance fee, morning coffee, lunches and afternoon tea are available opposite, at the Charlecote Pheasant Hotel (children welcome).

The Walk

Charlecote House is well worth visiting before your walk, and is just a short stroll from the main gates. The home of the Lucy family since 1247, the present Charlecote House was built in the 1550s by Sir Thomas Lucy, and later visited by Queen Elizabeth I, who spent two nights here in 1572. The story is often told that the young William Shakespeare was caught poaching Sir Thomas Lucy's deer in 1583, but there is no evidence to support this. The property was given to the National Trust in 1946 and the house is shown as it would have been over a century ago, after it was reconstructed in Elizabethan Revival style by George Hammond Lucy.

The park, which supports herds of red and fallow deer, and Britain's oldest flock of Jacob sheep, was landscaped by Capability

Deer in Charlecote Park with St Peter's Church, Hampton Lucy, beyond

Brown, who made good use of the mansion's setting by the Avon. Some enjoyable short walks are possible in the park.

Having explored house and grounds, and visited the tea room, leave by the main entrance and turn left beside the road. The deer park is on your left, and if the deer are grazing close by you will enjoy good views. Pass St Leonard's Church, built around 1850 in the Decorated style but all too obviously Victorian. It does contain some 17th-century monuments, moved from the old church which it replaced. One is the work of the aptly named Nicholas Stone, considered the finest 17th-century English sculptor.

Much more satisfying than St Leonard's is the view across the deer park to St Peter's at Hampton Lucy, a little to the north-west of Charlecote Park. This church stands on the site of an ancient Mercian minster church which was part of the estate of the Bishops of Worcester, who had a palace here in Saxon times. St Peter's is one of the earliest and best examples of a Gothic Revival church in England. It dates from 1826 and was designed by Thomas Rickman, though the polygonal apse at the east end was added by Sir Gilbert Scott in 1856. The great east window depicting the life of St Peter was described in the 19th century as "the most magnificent window in stained glass that has been produced in modern times".

At a road junction, turn left towards Hampton Lucy. After crossing the two channels of the Avon at the edge of the village, turn right on a bridleway which is also the private drive to Avonford Cottage. Just before you reach the cottage the bridleway makes a slight left turn to detour around the property. It then climbs gently to the top of a partially tree-clad cliff which provides fine views over the Avon Valley.

Reaching open grassland, keep on in the same direction. Before long the bridleway returns briefly into the trees before emerging again. Ahead of you the town of Warwick is clearly visible, dominated by church and castle. To your left is Monument Hill at Welcombe, Stratford.

A stile on the right gives access to an area of land open under the Countryside Stewardship scheme, so feel free to explore if you wish. Otherwise, just continue on the bridleway, which follows an obvious course across fields.

When you come to an area of scrub close to the highest point of Copdock Hill (only 282ft/86m), the bridleway bears right to keep close to the edge and affords another excellent viewpoint. To your left is the trig point, partially concealed by vegetation. Just keep following the waymarked bridleway until eventually you descend to a lane. Turn left, and left again at each subsequent junction to return to Charlecote by way of Hampton Lucy, where you may wish to spare a few minutes to visit St Peter's Church.

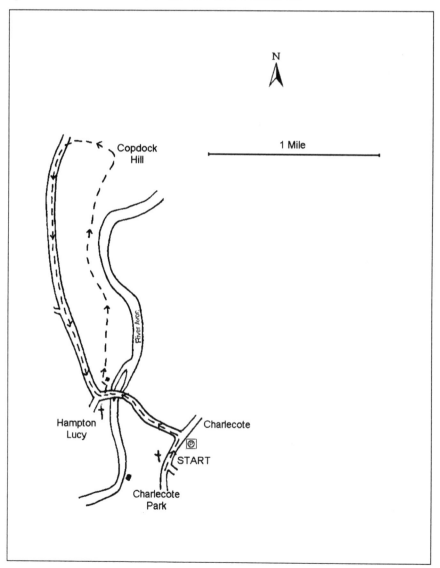

Walk 11: The Dene Valley

Start: Kineton, grid reference 336510.

Finish: Wellesbourne, grid reference 277552.

Summary: This delightful linear walk includes the beautiful village of Combrook and some excellent bridleways through lovely countryside. You can expect to see lots of wildlife, including deer if you're lucky, and birds such as jays, pheasants and buzzards. It's mostly on level ground, with well-defined paths and about 15 stiles. Kineton is easily reached by bus from Stratford.

Length: 8 miles/12.8km.

Maps: OS Landranger 151, OS Pathfinder 998.

Buses/Coaches: Stagecoach Midland Red 18/X18 Stratford to Coventry via Wellesbourne, daily; 270 Stratford to Banbury via Wellesbourne and/or Kineton, Monday to Saturday; 274 Stratford to Leamington via Wellesbourne and Kineton, Monday to Saturday; 502 Banbury to Kineton, Thursdays and Saturdays; Catteralls Coaches from Cubbington and Warwick to Wellesbourne, Tuesdays.

Trains: Nearest station is Stratford.

Parking: In Stratford, Kineton or Wellesbourne.

The Tea Shop
Wellesbourne Watermill, Kineton Road, Wellesbourne.

This is a working mill, open to the public and attractively set in the leafy Dene Valley. Close by is an 18th-century barn which now serves as the tea shop. Its walls are hung with old tools and farming implements as well as paintings by local artists, creating a pleasant atmosphere in which to enjoy a treat from the extensive menu. This includes tea, coffee, chocolate and cold drinks, with cakes, soups, rolls, sandwiches and quiches. Scones come in a variety of imaginative flavours including apple and hazelnut. Soups are made with vegetable stock and a number of other choices are suitable for vegetarians. Also for sale are stoneground flour, fudge, preserves and a range of books and gifts, not to mention coracles – Shrewsbury-style, but made on the premises. The barn is spacious and there's also outdoor seating, at which you may be visited by a friendly grey cat. Dogs are welcome but may not be taken inside the tea shop or the mill.

Open: 10.00am-5.00pm Thursday to Sunday, Easter to end of September. Also Tuesday and Wednesday from the third week of July to end of August, and Sunday afternoons in October and March (and possibly throughout winter). Telephone: 01789 470237.

Shetland ponies by the River Dene at Wellesbourne Watermill

The Walk

Kineton was for centuries a market town of some importance, but is now just a large village. It's not overwhelmingly picturesque, but there are some attractive old cottages and a lovely ironstone church. From the bus stop by the church, walk the few paces to the main road and turn right, then right again down Manor Lane, which leads to the B4451, where you turn left. Just past Sycamore Court turn left again, to Little Kineton, where more attractive cottages are grouped around the village green.

There are three horse chestnut trees in the centre and just beyond them is the village pond and a sign for a footpath, which passes Green Cottage to enter a pasture. Cross to the other side and turn right along the edge of a paddock beside a belt of dense blackthorn scrub, heavy with sloes in early autumn. A footbridge and stile give access to a large arable field and you continue in the same direction, except that the hedge is now on your left.

Approaching a farm, join a track by a large, black barn and keep straight on through the farmyard. Pass in front of the farmhouse and the adjacent barn then swing left. As you approach a pair of thatched cottages, turn right to where a dilapidated gate and stile give access to pasture. Bear right towards a stile standing forlorn, bereft of either hedge or fence, in the middle of the field, then continue in the same direction to a stile which gives access to a lane at Butlers Marston. Turn left towards the parish church, an attractive building with a mellow ironstone tower.

Exit the churchyard at the far side and walk to the road. Cross over and go up the lane opposite. When you reach a former Wesleyan chapel which has been converted into a house, turn left on a bridleway. After a fenced section it joins a concrete track, where you turn right. The surrounding countryside takes on a gently undulating feel now, as you descend to pass a sewage works by the River Dene, after which the bridleway continues as a grassy track. A stile and gate lead into cattle pasture and you go straight across to the other side. Continue across an arable field, bearing left to where the hedge opposite begins to swing away a little. A bridle gate is hidden here, under an oak tree. Turn left in the next field and follow its edge until you meet another bridleway, where you turn right. In places this is a tree-lined green lane, elsewhere just a field-edge track, but the route is never in doubt, and there are good views of the wooded Dene Valley, while plum, hawthorn, wild rose, elder and bramble line the bridleway itself.

After passing Oxhouse Farm the bridleway bears left as a surfaced track and you eventually arrive at an unsigned gate on the right. Pass through and go diagonally left to a footbridge spanning the Dene. Having crossed, bear left across a field, heading for a small bridle gate. Cross a dismantled railway, go through another bridle gate and turn right, following waymarks towards a farm and then left. The bridleway is easy to follow now, a wide track along the edges of woodland and fields.

Reaching Combrook, the onward route is to the left, along a lane, but first it's worth exploring the village, a delightful, secluded place deep in the wooded valley of the Com Brook. Resuming the walk, follow the lane uphill to the main road, the Fosse Way. Turn left then cross to an unsigned bridleway which forms the access track to Hyldewood Kennels, descending beside woodland to a major junction. Don't turn left here, towards Hyldewood, but go straight on, just to the right of a ditch.

Entering Roundhill Wood, the bridleway is now well-defined.

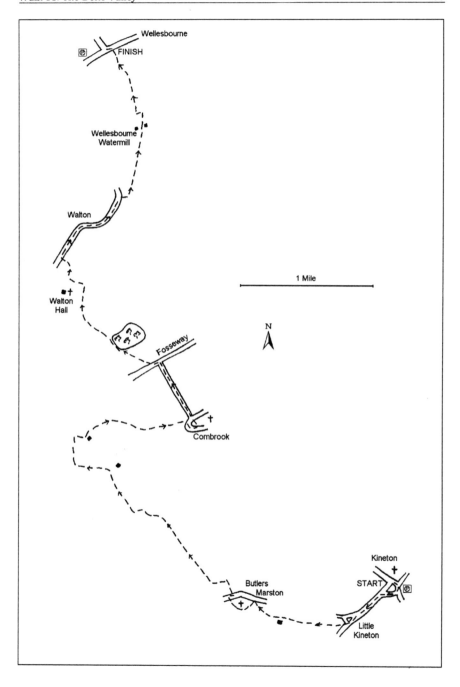

This lovely oak wood has a substrata of field maple, hawthorn, wild privet and willows. The latter flourish alongside the stream on your left, and the wood has a wonderfully tangled, jungly feel about it, rare in Warwickshire. After leaving the wood, cross a bridge to reach an arable field. Across the field, up a slope, is more woodland, with a track running along the edge of it. Go diagonally left to meet this track and turn left along it.

A large mansion set in parkland comes into view – this is Walton Hall Hotel, a massive Gothic pile built by Sir Gilbert Scott in the 1850s for the Mordaunt family. Go through a pair of gates and turn right towards the hotel. Having passed some modern, red-brick buildings, continue forward across playing fields to meet a track, where you turn left. When you see an 18th-century chapel turn right, approaching a reed-fringed, lily-padded lake formed by a small dam across the River Dene. You are likely to see dozens, maybe hundreds, of Canada geese here, as well as mallards, moorhens and swans. Cross the lake on a balustraded bridge.

At the road turn right to walk through Walton, formerly known as Walton d'Eivile. Here, attractive estate cottages, also designed by Scott, bear depressing names such as The Old Post Office and The Old Forge, where "old" means former rather than ancient, hammering home how rural services have declined over the last 40 years.

When you come to a ford and footbridge, cross the River Dene and walk forward up a track for a few paces before climbing a stile on the left to join a footpath, which follows field edges to the Mill Farm and Wellesbourne Watermill. The mill (admission charge) is to the left, the tea room to the right. After leaving the tea room, climb a stile into a paddock and go straight across this and the next. At the far side turn left to a footbridge over the river. Cross the bridge then turn right along the field edge to a stile. Continue the length of another field then along an enclosed path into Wellesbourne.

This large, busy place was once two villages, one on either side of the River Dene: Wellesbourne Hastings and Wellesbourne Mountford. The two have not only merged but also been submerged in the suburban flood. Turn right, then left, along a very pleasant street (Chapel Street), leading to the lovely 18th-century houses of Chestnut Square, the relatively unspoilt centre of Wellesbourne. There are bus stops here for Stratford, Warwick, Leamington, Coventry etc., though you might like to explore further before leaving. There are some pleasant houses on Church Walk, but the church itself is mainly Victorian, though not without interest.

Walk 12: Alcester, Exhall and Wixford

Start/finish: High Street, Alcester; grid reference 090575.

Summary: This undemanding circular walk from Warwickshire's most attractive small town takes you into a mixture of wooded and arable countryside, includes the chance to explore a remnant of the Forest of Arden and visits two small villages immortalised by Shakespeare (allegedly!).

Length: 5½ miles/8.8km.

Maps: OS Landranger 150, OS Pathfinder 997.

Buses/Coaches: Stagecoach Midland Red 25/26 Stratford to Redditch via Alcester, Monday to Saturday; First Midland Red 146/176 Birmingham to Evesham via Alcester, Monday to Saturday; Johnsons Henley to Redditch via Alcester, Thursdays; Cambridge Coach Services 71 Bromsgrove and/or Worcester to Cambridge via Alcester, daily; National Express 480 Kidderminster to London via Alcester, daily.

Trains: Nearest stations are Wootton Wawen and Wilmcote.

Parking: Public car parks in Alcester.

The Tea Shop

Tudor Rose Tea Rooms and Restaurant, 9 High Street, Alcester.

The timber-framed building now housing Tudor Rose Tea Rooms dates from 1512. The heavily beamed and partially panelled interior is warm, cosy and furnished in traditional style, its most striking feature the low ceiling with decorative plasterwork (said to be original) which features a Tudor rose and heraldic shields. In this attractive setting you can choose from a comprehensive menu of meals and light snacks and the usual range of hot and cold drinks. The choice of cakes is particularly tempting and many items on the menu are suitable for vegetarians. Smoking is permitted but not encouraged – ashtrays are supplied only on request. Dogs are made welcome, and this tea shop is already popular with walkers.

Open: 9.00am-6.00pm daily. Telephone: 01789 763025.

Malt Mill Lane, Alcester

The Walk

Alcester stands at the confluence of the Arrow and the Alne, and is a place of great antiquity: archaeological evidence indicates the site has been populated for over 12 000 years. It seems to have prospered throughout much of its history, especially from the 16th century onwards, when it became an important centre for the wool and linen trades, also for malting, ironworking and the cottage industry of needle-making. Throughout the 18th and 19th centuries, Alcester continued to grow in status as a market town, and also as an important staging point on coach routes to London. It is crammed with buildings of architectural merit and charm: there are fine examples of medieval and Tudor timber-framing in the High Street and a particularly good group of Georgian houses in Henley Street. The church, however, was mostly rebuilt in the 18th century and is of only moderate interest, apart from some fine memorials.

Walk along High Street towards the church and follow the road round, turning right on the Heart of England Way, which takes you down lovely Malt Mill Lane, lined with buildings spanning four centuries. As the lane bends right, turn left by a horse chestnut tree and follow the River Arrow to the new Stratford road. Cross and turn left along the old road. Cross the river into Oversley Green and turn right

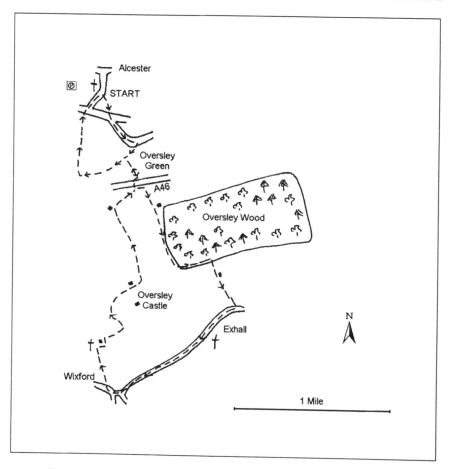

on Mill Lane, passing timber-framed houses to reach Primrose Lane, where you turn left. This takes you across the bypass (using a footbridge) to Primrose Hill, where you join a bridleway (the Arden Way) on the left. It soon makes a right turn and climbs gently, passing to the right of Summerhill House and on along the edge of Oversley Wood.

Of Warwickshire's once great Forest of Arden, only tiny remnants now survive, islanded in a sea of intensive agriculture. Of these, Oversley Wood is one of the largest and, although planted with conifers by the Forestry Commission, it does maintain considerable interest. The route described here offers only glimpses of the wood, but there are several points at which you can gain access if you wish.

It's inhabited by roe deer and a range of other wildlife. If you're lucky you may see deer on the bridleway, especially early in the day.

The Marquess of Hertford's home, 17th-century Ragley Hall (open to the public), is visible to the west, and so is the rather smaller Oversley Castle, a white-painted, embattled folly built to please the Prince Regent, a close friend of an earlier Marquess and, it was rumoured, an even closer friend of the Marchioness. The Prince commented that the view from the Hall would be enhanced by the addition of a "castle", and so one was built.

Emerge at a path junction next to arable fields and turn left, still on the bridleway, which now follows the inner edge of the wood. When you again emerge from the trees, the bridleway makes a right turn along the edge of a field. Pass Rosehall Farm as the bridleway descends towards a lane. Turn right through Exhall, a small village described, possibly by Shakespeare, as "dodging Exhall" in an oft-quoted doggerel verse attributed to him, though there is no real evidence that he wrote it. The story is that after a heavy drinking bout the hungover Bard vowed never again to drink with the men of:

> Piping Pebworth, dancing Marston,
> Haunted Hillborough, hungry Grafton,
> Dodging Exhall, Papist Wixford,
> Beggarly Broom and drunken Bidford.

Why "dodging Exhall"? It is usually suggested that this refers to the fragmented nature of the village, but surely there's a more interesting explanation?

Keep going along the lane to reach a road. Make three consecutive right turns to join a "no through road" to Wixford Church. This lovely lane is now little more than a track, bordered by tall hedges which meet overhead, but it was once part of the Roman road known as Ryknild Street. "Papist Wixford" is so-named because the manor was owned from 1541 by the Roman Catholic Throckmorton family of Coughton Court (see Walk 13). The church, St Milburga's, is of the 11th century, though much restored.

Opposite the entrance to St Milburga's is a waymarked post. Rejoin the Heart of England Way here, and it will take you past Oversley Farm and then round the side of the hill crowned by Oversley Castle before turning left to reach Lower Oversley Lodge. Turn right along a track to the footbridge across the bypass. Return along Primrose Lane to Mill Lane then turn left. Use the footbridge to cross the river and join Bleachfield Street (where linen was bleached in the Middle Ages). This leads back to the High Street.

Walk 13: Alcester and Coughton

Start/finish: High Street, Alcester; grid reference 090575.

Summary: An easy circular walk, mostly on level ground but with a couple of gentle slopes. It explores farmland, woodland and the River Arrow, and features the architecturally and historically interesting Coughton Court.

Length: 8½ miles/13.6km.

Maps: OS Landranger 150, OS Pathfinders 975 and 997.

Buses/Coaches: Stagecoach Midland Red 25/26 Stratford to Redditch via Alcester, Monday to Saturday; First Midland Red 146/176 Birmingham to Evesham via Alcester, Monday to Saturday; Johnsons Henley to Redditch via Alcester, Thursdays; Cambridge Coach Services 71 Bromsgrove and/or Worcester to Cambridge via Alcester, daily; National Express 480 Kidderminster to London via Alcester, daily.

Trains: Nearest stations are Wootton Wawen and Wilmcote.

Parking: Public car parks in Alcester.

The Tea Shop

Whitehead's Home Bakery, 67 High Street, Alcester.

Situated at the southern end of High Street, at its junction with Swan Street, Whitehead's is not only conveniently located but also bright, cheerful, welcoming and friendly. Owners Brett and Anita Hellyer provide a wide range of bread, cakes, pastries and savouries, all baked on the premises and all superb value. Also available are fresh sandwiches and rolls, home-made soup, baguettes with salad and jackets with various fillings, all complemented by a range of hot and cold drinks. Vegetarians will be able to find something suitable but should ask for details. Dogs are not allowed in the tea room but they are welcome to stay in the yard and will be provided with water.

Open: 9.00am-5.00pm Monday to Saturday. Telephone: 01789 762647.

The Walk

Standing with your back to High Street, turn right on Swan Street. At the roundabout go straight on along Seggs Lane, which subsequently becomes Allimore Lane and takes you across the bypass (on

Bovine companions you may encounter on this walk

a footbridge). A little further on you reach the entrance to Coldcom-fort Farm, where you bear right on a track. Ignoring any branching paths, just keep forward to enter Coldcomfort Wood, a mixture of conifers and native species, all draped with wild honeysuckle.

The path climbs gently between the trees to a junction, where you keep straight on to eventually leave the wood at a gate. Continue across fields, more or less straight on, then by the side of a wide hedge to a junction. Go left to pass a plantation and reach the road at Cookhill. Cross to a footpath opposite which leads to a small group of houses where you turn right, past a partially timber-framed cottage. When you reach a track, cross to a footpath a little on the left and just keep going in the same direction, soon joining Cladswell Lane. Join the first footpath on the right, following the right-hand edge of a field to a stile then going diagonally to the far left corner of a second field to reach Evesham Road. Turn left and cross to a bridleway signed to Alcester Heath. Descend a bank to a fence and gate then turn right to find another gate. Go through and keep straight ahead on a hedged track before turning left to pass Alcester Park Farm. When you reach a galvanised gate join the farm track and continue in the same direction. As you approach a small brick building,

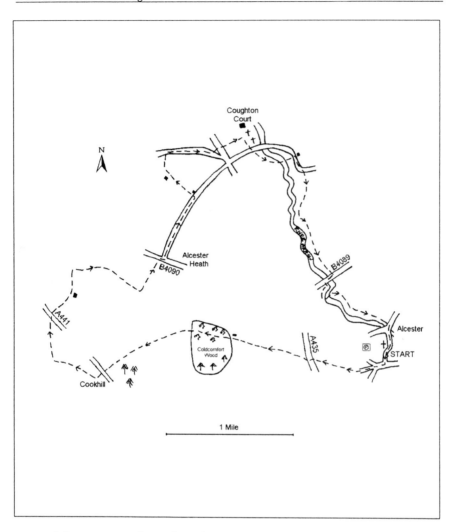

turn right over a stile and go forward along the edge of a field. After passing a pool, cross to the other side of the hedge but keep on in much the same direction to the field corner then turn left on a bridleway to the road.

Turn right and cross to Coughton Lane. After just over half a mile join a footpath on the left, next to a brick house. Keep straight on, passing to the right of a farm, Coughton Lodge, then turning right on the farm access track to pass between tree-covered earthworks which mark the position of an ancient moat, now dry. Joining Sambourne Lane, turn right and continue almost to the point at which it joins the main road. Shortly before it does so, take a footpath on the left, just after passing Spiney House. The footpath leads to the road, where you join another path opposite, heading for Coughton Court across parkland grazed by Jacob sheep.

The Court has been home for nearly 600 years to the Throckmortons, who were originally from the eponymous Worcestershire village. They acquired Coughton in 1409 when John Throckmorton married a member of the Spiney family, who had owned the manor since 1280. The Throckmortons feature in English history on many occasions, chiefly because they mostly remained staunch Roman Catholics after the Reformation, which inevitably set them against the authorities. There was a Throckmorton plot against Elizabeth I in 1583, following which Francis Throckmorton was tortured and executed, and the family also had some involvement in the Gunpowder Plot of 1605. Not all the Throckmortons were Catholics: in 1554 Nicholas Throckmorton, a Protestant, was involved in Wyatt's Rebellion against Mary Tudor; and in 1598 Job Throckmorton, a Puritan, was arrested under suspicion of being "Martin Marprelate", author of scurrilous tracts critical of priests and bishops. At least one member of the family was involved in romantic rather than religious intrigue: Bessie Throckmorton, a maid of honour to Elizabeth, became Sir Walter Raleigh's secret bride in 1592. When the Queen found out both were sent to the Tower. But not all the Throckmortons were out of step with authority – in the 15th century John Throckmorton was Under Treasurer of England and London's Throgmorton Street is named after him.

Though Coughton Court now belongs to the National Trust and is open to the public, the Throckmorton family lives there still. The Court has a magnificent Tudor gatehouse and half-timbered courtyard and is set in beautiful parkland. Close by is St Peter's Church, which dates mainly from the time of Sir Robert Throckmorton (1468-1518). It has many fine features and some interesting tombs – don't miss the intriguing memorial to Henry Teong and Elizabeth Dewes, who died in 1681 and are apparently buried together.

Leaving the churchyard, turn left, soon passing another church, a Roman Catholic one dedicated to St Peter, St Paul and St Elizabeth. This was built by the Throckmortons in 1856, some 27 years after Catholic emancipation.

Leaving Coughton Park, cross a lane to find two waymarked footpaths opposite. Take the left-hand one, following the River Arrow across two fields to a lane. Turn right past Milford Farm and at the entrance to Church Farm, climb a stile into a field and walk to the far right corner. Entering another field, head towards the river and follow it to a road on the edge of Alcester. Turn right, crossing both the river and the road to find a flight of steps descending to fields. Turn right, again beside the Arrow. When you come to a junction, turn left over a former railway bridge and then turn right through a picnic area to rejoin the river. It remains a close companion as you skirt farmland and playing fields to reach Kinwarton Road. Turn right into Alcester.

Walk 14: Henley-in-Arden and Bannam's Wood

Start/finish: Henley-in-Arden Station, grid reference 148659.

Summary: An undemanding circular walk in mixed farmland in an area popular with local walkers. It provides some lovely views over the countryside and the opportunity to explore the attractive little town of Henley. The paths are easy to follow but there are about 20 stiles to clamber over.

Length: 6 miles/9.6km.

Maps: OS Landranger 139 and 151, OS Pathfinder 975.

Buses/Coaches: Stagecoach Midland Red X50 Birmingham to Oxford via Henley, daily.

Trains: Central Trains Stratford to Worcester via Henley, daily.

Parking: Public car parks in Henley.

The Tea Shop

Henley Café, 97 High Street, Henley-in-Arden.

A forest of oak beams provides an attractive backdrop for lots of round tables with cheerful green and yellow tablecloths, and an array of local prints on the walls. Baskets overflowing with plants are suspended from the beams, and there are more floral displays outside. There is plenty of outside seating too, both at the front by the road and also in a pleasant garden at the back. A very wide range of goodies is on offer, including all-day breakfasts, soups, the Henley Bap (with a choice of fillings), sandwiches, snacks on toast, grills, jackets, pasta dishes, omelettes and salads. There are the traditional tea shop favourites including tea cakes, crumpets, scones, cakes, puddings and desserts, and the usual range of drinks. Some meals are suitable for vegetarians, with free-range eggs, for instance, usually available. Special children's meals are provided, and also the famous Henley ice cream, with flavours ranging from caramel and cashew nut to kirsch and black cherry.

  Open: 10.00am-5.00pm Monday to Friday; 9.00am-5.00pm Saturday; 11.00am-5.00pm Sunday. Telephone: 01564 792135.

The Walk

Shakespeare's Forest of Arden now exists in name only, but there is still plenty of lovely countryside in the area once covered by the forest. It's a gently undulating landscape, with small fields and copses and ancient hedges. In the centre of it all lies Henley-in-Arden, a busy little town strung out along the A3400, though the never-ending traffic can't altogether destroy the charm of its timber-framed frontages, bright with flowers throughout the summer.

Henley first developed under the protection of Beaudesert, a 12th-century castle built by Thurstan de Montfort, whose famous namesake Simon de Montfort (no relation) led a revolt against Henry III and lost his life at the Battle of Evesham in 1265. After the battle, the town which had grown up around the castle was destroyed and subsequent development took place along what is now High Street. Only a large, steep mound marks the castle site today. Below the mound is the largely Norman church of Beaudesert, while a short distance away on High Street is Henley's own church, a 15th-century building of grey stone. Next to it the timber-framed former Guild Hall, now the library,

High Street, Henley

also dates from the 15th century, and there are many other buildings of great interest lining the High Street.

The outward leg of the walk makes use of the Heart of England Way, which crosses the railway at Henley by means of a footbridge. (If starting from the town centre you can reach the station via Shallowford Court or Bear Lane.) Having descended the steps on the far side of the line, go straight on, past allotments, until you come to a junction, where you turn left. Cross a footbridge and go forward over sheep pasture to meet the main road.

Cross over and pass close by Well Cottage. Three stiles lead into pastureland and you go straight across, still on the Heart of England Way. Just keep following the waymarks and you can't go wrong as the path leads you over a mixture of arable and pasture. When you come to a lane the path continues on the other side, climbing up towards woodland.

This is Bannam's Wood, and although there is a public footpath through it, another path has been negotiated on a concessionary basis, running just outside its eastern edge, supposedly to protect the ecology of the wood, which is an SSSI (Site of Special Scientific Interest). This is the route taken by the Heart of England Way and it does have some advantages, providing far-reaching views which are not available from within Bannam's Wood. During April, May and June, if you have a dog with you, it's requested that you keep it on the lead to avoid disturbing ground-nesting birds and their young.

The path eventually descends through trees to reach a gate, where the Heart of England way makes a right turn. Turn left instead, on a bridleway. Though it is not waymarked, a series of short, white posts indicates the route at first, after which it becomes an obvious track.

Near Upper Wawensmoor Farm the bridleway acquires a hard surface as it merges with a "no through road". This takes you to the main road, where you turn right for about 250 metres before crossing to a footpath.

The path follows a clear course until a gate is reached. Go through and continue in much the same direction but with a hedge now on your right. When the hedge bends to the right, veer away from it and walk to a stile visible ahead in the left-hand corner of the field.

Walk straight ahead to cross another stile and then turn right, following the right-hand hedge to join a track which leads to May's Farm. After passing a pond, bear slightly right away from the track,

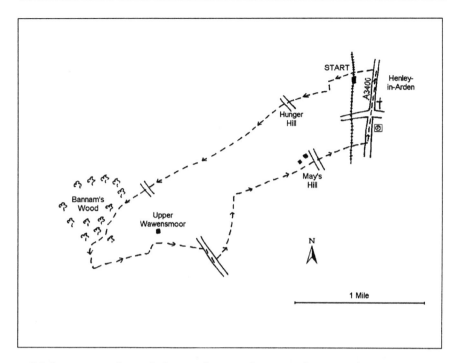

which soon makes a left turn by another pond. Keep close to a fence on the right so that you bypass the farm to reach a road at May's Hill.

Cross to another footpath opposite and go straight on past a group of ash trees then by a straggly row of hawthorns to a stile. Cross another field, pass to the left of some barns and continue to a gate near a phone box. Just keep straight on to reach the main road at the southern end of Henley and turn left to return to your starting point.

Walk 15: Henley-in-Arden and Preston Bagot

Start/finish: Henley-in-Arden Station, grid reference 148659.

Summary: Some of the most charming countryside in Warwickshire is explored in this easy circular walk which takes you over the earthworks of Beaudesert Castle then across gently undulating countryside to a particularly lovely stretch of the Stratford Canal before returning via the hilltop hamlet of Preston Bagot.

Length: 6 miles/9.6km.

Maps: OS Landranger 151, OS Pathfinder 975.

Buses/Coaches: Stagecoach Midland Red X50 Birmingham to Oxford via Henley, daily.

Trains: Central Trains Stratford to Worcester via Henley, daily.

Parking: Public car parks in Henley.

The Tea Shop

Henley Ice Cream Parlour, High Street, Henley-in-Arden.

Henley Ice Cream has been produced in Warwickshire for over 60 years and is available in the most tempting range of flavours: the ice cream parlour on High Street is the ideal place to sample it in comfort. Just look for the distinctive and colourful Henley Ice Cream sign – a cow jumping over a crescent moon against the backdrop of a starry sky – projecting from a striking, timber-framed building next to the Heritage Centre at the southern end of High Street. Heavily beamed inside, with old black and white photographs on the walls, the ice cream parlour is still light, bright and fresh, with a relaxed atmosphere. It offers the range of ices and sundaes (including chocolate indulgence, fruit explosion and Knickerbocker Glory) you would expect, but also a variety of tea shop staples, such as sandwiches, scones and cakes. Some items are suitable for vegetarians (veggie cheese is used for sandwiches), there are plenty of hot and cold drinks to choose from and there is some outside seating for warm days. Guide dogs are welcome.

Open: 10.00am-8.00pm daily, June to August; 10.00am-5.00pm daily, September to May. Telephone: 01564 792141.

The Walk

For details of Henley, see Walk 14. This walk also uses a stretch of the Heart of England Way, which you can join at the station and follow to the High Street. At St John the Baptist's Church turn on to a narrow lane, soon passing St Nicholas's Church to reach Beaudesert Mount, the substantial earthwork which is all that remains of a motte and bailey castle built by Thurstan de Montfort in the 12th century.

A later de Montfort, Peter, became custodian of the castle in 1216, and eventually joined the growing opposition of the barons to King Henry III led by Peter's namesake, Simon de Montfort (no relation). In 1258 the barons forced reforms on Henry, and in 1265 they called England's first Parliament, in which Peter served as Speaker. Later

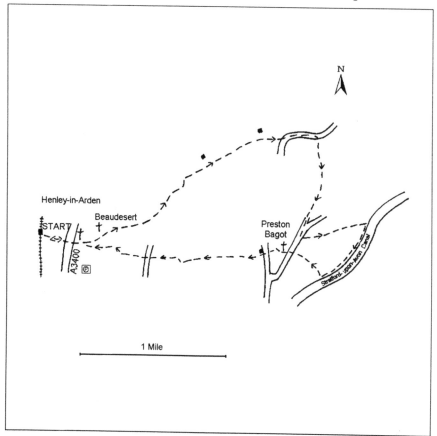

that year, however, the king triumphed at the Battle of Evesham, where both de Montforts died.

Walk over the top of the Mount and forward, towards a ridge opposite. At the top of the ridge, turn left over a stile and follow a path along the edge of a field, with a hawthorn hedge on your right. Look out for another stile on the right, and after crossing it go diagonally left to the far corner of a field. Climb another stile and turn left along Edge Lane, a green lane once used by the Romans but probably already in existence long before their time. Today it is lined with a splendid tangle of blackthorn, elder and wild rose. All too soon you have to leave it, turning right into a field. Follow a well-trodden path across it and keep going in much the same direction across several fields and through a small copse. Pass Hungerfield Farm and Holly Bank Farm to eventually reach a lane close to the latter. The path is clear all the way.

Turn left along the lane as far as Willowbrook House, where you leave the Heart of England Way as you turn right on to a "no through road" known as Preston Field Lane, a lovely old track bordered by some fine pollarded willows rising from a tangled understorey of other greenery.

All too soon, the track becomes a metalled lane, passing between houses. At a junction with another lane, keep on in the same direction for about 120 metres then climb a stile on the left and follow a hedged path to enter a pasture. Continue forward in the same direction along field edges, until a stile on the right gives access to a footbridge. After crossing this go very slightly right across a boggy field to the far side, where you'll see a gate to the right of a clump of alders. Continue towards a house, just beyond which a stile gives on to a flight of steps to Yarningale Aqueduct, which carries the Stratford Canal over a brook. This is the smallest of three aqueducts along the canal, and is simple, but effective, in design, just a basic trough formed from bolted iron plates and supported by brick piers.

Turn right on the towpath, along what is a particularly leafy and lovely section of the Stratford Canal. When you reach lock 36, leave the towpath, joining a footpath on the right which takes you across a stream then up the left-hand edge of a field and forward through another field to a lane. Cross to a path opposite which passes Preston Bagot's small, partially Norman church, standing proud on top of a knoll with far-reaching views across Arden.

The path then descends to a lane and passes Church Farm to enter meadowland. Keep straight on at all junctions until you meet an overgrown green lane. Turn right along here but only for a few metres, until a stile on the left allows you to regain your heading.

Reaching Edge Lane again (though this section is metalled), join a footpath almost opposite which takes you to the top of the ridge then drops steeply down to cross a recreation ground and reach a residential area. Go straight on to the bottom of Beaudesert Mound and turn left into Henley.

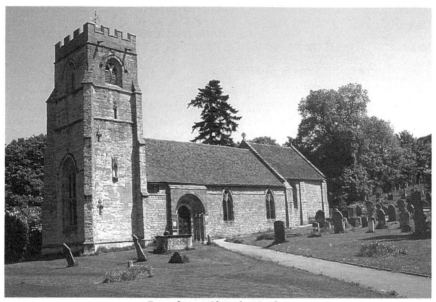

Beaudesert Church, Henley

Walk 16: Wootton Wawen

Start/finish: Wootton Wawen Station, grid reference 149631.

Summary: A longish circular walk, but a relatively undemanding one as the terrain is mostly very gentle. It includes the pretty village of Aston Cantlow, a delightful stretch of the Stratford Canal and, unexpectedly, England's longest aqueduct. Wootton Wawen itself is of considerable interest but suffers from its position astride the main road.

Length: 9 miles/14.5km.

Maps: OS Landranger 151, OS Pathfinder 975.

Buses/Coaches: Stagecoach Midland Red X50 Birmingham to Oxford via Wootton Wawen, daily.

Trains: Central Trains Stratford to Worcester via Wootton Wawen, daily except Sundays. (The trains do run on Sundays but they don't stop at Wootton Wawen. They do stop at nearby Henley, however, from where the X50 provides a link.)

Parking: Some roadside parking may be available in Wootton Wawen. Alternatively, you can leave a car at Yew Tree Farm if there is room – ask permission first. There is also a parking space near the junction of Pettiford Lane and Green Lane at grid reference 161637.

The Tea Shop
The Heron's Nest, Yew Tree Farm Craft Centre, Wootton Wawen.

Yew Tree Farm is an elegant Georgian farmhouse with a fine collection of outbuildings, and you'll find it on the south-east edge of Wootton Wawen at the junction of the A3400 with Pettiford Lane, close to the aqueduct which carries the Stratford Canal across the main road. The former stableyard has been converted into units selling antiques, crafts and a variety of other goods, and another unit houses the Heron's Nest. The heavily beamed room has a gallery floor at one end and is beautifully fitted out with substantial pine furniture and decorated with local artwork. The menu lists a variety of snacks and salads, in addition to the more traditional teacakes, crumpets, scones and cakes. Children's portions are available and there is a limited vegetarian selection. The range of drinks is not so wide as some, but does include such wicked treats as hot chocolate with marshmallows. There is also outside seating in a small garden and dogs are welcome here, but not indoors.

Open: 10.00am-5.00pm Tuesday to Sunday. Telephone: 01564 792979.

The Walk

If you're starting from the station, it's just a short walk by the B4089 into the centre of Wootton Wawen. The village, set in the valley of the River Alne, has several attractive houses and a 14th-century pub. St Peter's Church is one of Warwickshire's most interesting, and possibly its oldest. It was founded around 730 and served as a minster church. A substantial amount of Saxon masonry survives and there is work from every other medieval period.

Nearby Wootton Hall is a fine 17th-century mansion which once belonged to Mrs Maria Fitzherbert, the most enduring of George IV's mistresses. It is believed that he entered into a secret marriage with her in 1785 but they parted in 1803. The hall stands in fine parkland with an ornamental lake, and, incongruously, a caravan site.

Walking towards Stratford along the main road, you soon come to Yew Tree Farm, on the corner of Pettiford Lane, where you turn left. (You may first wish to look at Wootton Wawen Aqueduct, just a few metres ahead – there is an unofficial path up to it.)

Wootton Hall

Walk up Pettiford Lane until you see a bridleway, Green Lane, on the right, and follow this lovely, old track through trees, soon crossing the canal. For a while the track is bordered by oak trees rising from a tangled understorey of smaller species, but then it enters woodland proper as it takes you through Austy Wood.

As you approach the far side of the wood you'll see an unsigned track branching right – ignore this but continue only a few paces further to find a waymarked footpath also going right. After about 300 metres on this path, look for a marker post concealed in vegetation on the right and turn left through Scots pines. The path soon leaves the wood and you continue along its edge until you come to a waymarker directing you through trees to the A3400.

Turn left, crossing over to the other side where there's a bit of a footway. When you reach the entrance to Silsbourne Rise, join a track and follow it as far as the canal. Here you join the towpath and turn left underneath bridge 56.

You soon pass over Edstone (also known as Bearley) Aqueduct, which carries the canal across the railway, a road and a brook. A cast-iron trough supported on thirteen brick piers, it is, at 754ft (230 m), the longest canal aqueduct in England, and easily the most dramatic engineering feature of the Stratford Canal.

At the next bridge (Draper Bridge) cross into a field and go right along the edge. After 300 metres go over a stile on the right and forward to another stile into the next field. Next go diagonally right to a stile in a fence. Keep the same heading across the next field, join a lane and turn left through the hamlet of Newnham, once a populous quarrying village. Ignore any turnings and follow the lane past Lower Farm, after which it becomes a bridleway, soon bending left.

Clearly defined, the bridleway runs by the hedge at first before turning right across fields. It eventually descends steeply through woodland then takes to the fields once more before emerging in Aston Cantlow. Turn left and note Chapel Lane on the right – this is the way back to Wootton Wawen, but first you'll probably want to walk into the village centre, where mellow brick cottages mingle happily with timbered ones. One of the finest buildings is the timber-framed pub, the 16th-century King's Head, which has been in the same family for many generations, while opposite it is another timber-framed building, the Guild House, also of the 16th century. A religious order, the Guild of St Mary, licensed in 1469, was based here.

Though only a small village today, Aston could have turned out

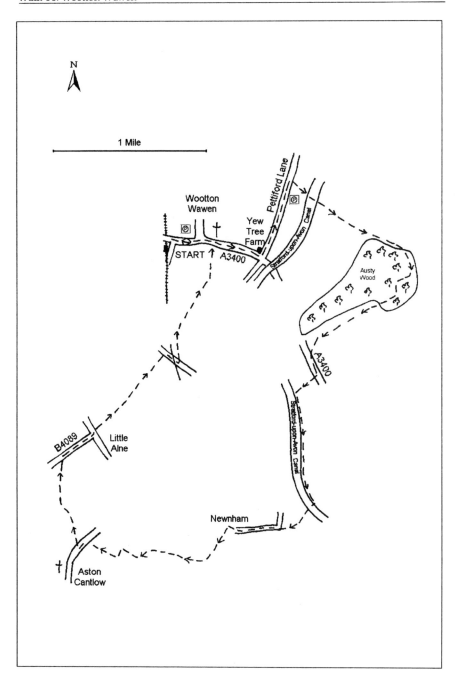

very differently. A castle was built here soon after the Conquest, and in 1227 the Lord of the Manor, William de Cantilupe, gained a royal charter for a weekly market and annual fair. But there were other markets within a few miles, at Henley, Stratford, Bidford and Alcester, all on good roads, and Aston Cantlow could not compete. The castle was destroyed by the king's forces after the Barons' War, in which Cantilupe had been a close supporter of the de Montforts (see Walks 14 and 15). Today only earthworks remain, on a site close to the River Alne. Stone from the castle may have been used in the building of St John the Baptist's Church, which dates from the 13th century.

Another de Cantilupe, Thomas, was the priest here for a time but became Bishop of Hereford in 1275 and was later canonised. Aston Cantlow is one of only two English parishes which can claim to have had a saint as parish priest. Tradition claims that John Shakespeare of Snitterfield and Mary Arden of Wilmcote were married at St John's in 1557 and celebrated their wedding at the King's Head. Fortunately for Aston, there is no documentary evidence, and without proof of the event, the village has been spared the tourist invasion.

Return to Chapel Lane to resume the walk. When the lane ends keep forward along a track to a stile. A footpath takes you across a dismantled railway into a field. Take the left-hand one of two paths and follow it across the River Alne then turn right beside the river. The path leads to the B4089, where you turn right on the Monarch's Way and go past the Arden Centre at Little Alne. At the main road junction, turn left towards Wootton Wawen for just a few metres – until you come to a footpath on the right. Walk forward across pasture, keeping close to the left-hand fence. Just keep straight on over Round Hill, soon descending to cross a stile. Turn left for a few metres then over another stile into a field and left again, still on the Monarch's Way. Pass to the left of a small, brick barn and continue in the same direction over the next field, keeping close to the river on your right.

Reaching the lane, turn right, pass under the railway, go left on a footpath and over a stile then bear right towards the river. Pass to the right of a sewage works and go on along a clear riverside path. You'll see two bridges – don't cross either of them but, at the second one, bear left on a footpath to Wootton Wawen and turn left to the station, or right to Yew Tree Farm.

🐾𝒲𝒶𝓁𝓀 17: 𝒦𝒾𝓃𝑔𝓈𝓌𝑜𝑜𝒹

Start/finish: Lapworth Station, grid reference 187716.

Summary: A medieval moated manor house belonging to the National Trust is the focus for this most enjoyable circular walk. It makes use of canal towpaths and the Heart of England Way, guaranteeing easy walking through attractive countryside. It also provides the opportunity to explore the recently restored Kingswood Junction, where the Stratford Canal meets the Grand Union Canal.

Length: 6 miles/9.6km.

Maps: OS Landranger 139, OS Pathfinders 954, 955, 975 and 976.

Buses/Coaches: Johnsons of Henley 62 Leamington to Solihull via Lapworth Station, Wednesdays and Fridays; Stagecoach Midland Red 61 Lowsonford to Warwick and Leamington via Lapworth Station, Wednesdays and Saturdays.

Trains: Central Trains Leamington to Worcester via Lapworth, daily; Chiltern Railways Birmingham to London via Lapworth, daily (change at Warwick or Leamington on Sundays).

Parking: Lapworth Station or picnic area off Brome Hall Lane, Kingswood. Alternatively, parking is available at Baddesley Clinton during opening hours, if visiting the property.

The Tea Shop
The Barn Restaurant, Baddesley Clinton Hall, Baddesley Clinton.

This pleasant tea room is situated in the spacious surroundings of a converted barn, one of a range of attractive, brick farm buildings around a grassed square, the former barnyard. Outside seating is also available. The menu includes a variety of hot lunch dishes, as well as soups, salads, ploughman's and puddings. There are set afternoon teas, with various combinations of scones, sandwiches and cakes. Vegetarians are catered for, and the soups are made with vegetable stock. No dogs are permitted except guide dogs.

Open: 12.00am-2.00pm and 2.30pm-5.30pm Wednesday to Sunday and Bank Holiday Mondays, March to end of October (closes at 5.00pm March, April and October); 12.00am-4.30pm Wednesday to Sunday, late February, November and early December. Telephone: 01564 783294.

Note: Baddesley Clinton is a National Trust property so an entrance fee is payable, except by Trust members, even if you intend only to visit the tea room. You can opt for a ticket to the grounds, restaurant and shop only, which is cheaper than an all-inclusive one. If you do wish to visit the house, note that parties of 15 or more require prior written arrangement.

The Walk

Leave Lapworth Station by way of a footbridge. Cross over platform two and descend steps to the west of the railway to join a footpath. A stile gives access to fields and a right turn leads to a lane. Turn left, taking care on a couple of blind bends, and walk as far as a bridge spanning the Stratford Canal. Join the towpath and turn right, under the bridge.

A series of locks leads to Kingswood Junction, where the Grand Union Canal and the Stratford Canal pass within 300 metres of each other, linked by a short arm. Completed in 1816, the Stratford Canal links Stratford with the Worcester and Birmingham Canal at King's Norton. It fell into disuse after it was taken over by the Great Western Railway in the 1850s, but was bought by the National Trust and restored by volunteers in the 1960s. In 1988 the Trust transferred ownership of the canal to British Waterways. The Stratford is notable for its unusual features, most of which – miniature locks, cast-iron split cantilever bridges and barrel-roofed cottages – are encountered on this walk.

Stay on the towpath of the Stratford Canal until you come to Dick's Lane, which crosses the canal on Bridge 39 by Kingswood Cottage. Turn left along the lane to reach a road then left again to Turner's Green Bridge, where you can join the towpath of the Grand Union Canal.

Turn right beside the Grand Union as far as Rowington Hill Bridge (62), join a lane and turn left, following the Heart of England Way to Rowington. Walk through the churchyard to a stile giving access to sheep pasture. Follow the waymarked route until you have passed a line of five mature oaks. There is a stile ahead at this point, but don't cross it. Turn left, leaving the Heart of England Way, and follow the hedge as far as the next big oak tree then go diagonally left towards the far corner of the field. Climb a stile and turn right through fields to reach a lane, then right again.

On reaching a road turn right then first left, rejoining the Heart of England Way. Now a clear bridleway, it leads through fields and along the edge of woodland to reach St Michael's Church at Baddesley Clinton, a lovely church in a lovely setting. It consists of a small nave, a chancel and an embattled tower. A one-time Lord of the Manor, Nicholas Brome, who died in 1517, was a double murderer and is buried in the church doorway, at his own penitent request, so that everyone entering the church must tread on his grave.

A tree-lined avenue leads from the churchyard to the entrance to Baddesley Clinton. This 15th-century house, set in fine gardens, is well worth a visit. Little changed since 1634, the house has a number

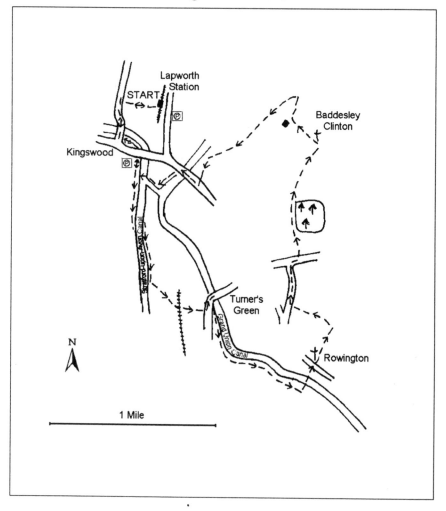

of intriguing priest holes created in the 1590s. It's a beautiful building, inside and out, full of character and atmosphere, with superb panelled rooms and a warm, lived-in feel about it. The grounds may be explored too, and include a a wildflower meadow, gardens, a lake and many parkland trees.

Whether or not you visit the house and tea room, continue on the Heart of England Way which leads along the driveway, which soon merges with another track. Leave the Way here, climbing a stile on the left into park-like pasture. Bear left so that you walk past the boundary of Baddesley Clinton and you'll come to a stile which takes you into farmland.

A field-edge path provides a clear route at first. As you approach a red-brick stable block, go diagonally right, passing under power lines, and heading towards a wooden fence. Aim to reach it about 100 metres north of the stables and climb over to join a track. Turn left, passing the stables and continuing to a road.

Turn right, crossing to a footway opposite, and walk to Kingswood Bridge, which spans the Grand Union Canal. Join the towpath and follow it south to the link with the Stratford Canal. Rejoin the Stratford towpath and retrace the route you used right at the beginning of the walk to return to Lapworth Station.

Kingswood Junction

Walk 18: Knowle

Start/finish: High Street, Knowle; grid reference 182768.

Summary: The focus of this easy circular walk through pleasant countryside is the delightful little settlement of Temple Balsall, as historically fascinating as it is picturesque. A short stretch of the Grand Union Canal adds further interest.

Length: 6½ miles/10.5km.

Maps: OS Landranger 139, OS Pathfinders 954 and 955.

Buses/Coaches: Travel West Midlands 38 Acocks Green to Dorridge via Knowle, Monday to Saturday; 39 Solihull to Dorridge via Knowle, Sundays; 40 Solihull to Knowle, Monday to Saturday; Caves 148/149 Dorridge circular via Knowle, Monday to Friday; 196/197 Solihull to Balsall Common via Knowle, Monday to Saturday; Arriva Midlands North 151 Hockley Heath to Solihull via Knowle, Monday to Saturday.

Trains: Nearest station is Dorridge (with frequent bus links).

Parking: Public car park in town centre.

The Tea Shop
Mad Hatter's Café Restaurant, 1628a High Street, Knowle.

This warm and cosy little place always extends a friendly welcome and offers an extensive menu from which to choose, ranging from the basic (faggots, chips and peas) to the more sophisticated (pâté, toast and salad). The snack menu includes all-day breakfasts, sandwiches, baguettes, egg and chips, scrambled eggs, sausages and chips, beans on toast, jacket potatoes and veggie burgers. If you want a more substantial meal you can choose from vegetable lasagne, chilli con carne, chicken goujons, battered prawns, and a range of daily specials. Vegetarians should have no trouble finding something suitable. Children's meals are available and, on Thursdays only, a good value roast lunch for senior citizens. Baked goods include teacakes, scones and a selection of home-made cakes and desserts. There is the usual selection of hot and cold drinks. A part of the tea room is set aside for smokers.

Open: 8.30am-5.00pm Monday to Saturday. Telephone: 01564 779806.

Almshouses at Temple Balsall

The Walk

Though perilously close to being engulfed by Solihull, Knowle remains a pleasant place with its own distinct character. After exploring the town centre, make your way towards the church at the end of High Street. Dedicated to St John the Baptist, St Lawrence and St Anne, it is a glorious building which was completed in 1402 in the Perpendicular style. It contains a great deal of fine carving, including some appealing misericords. Next to the church is the timber-framed Guild House, another architectural gem, which was built in 1412. It was the home of the Guild of St Anne of Knowle, but in later years served many other purposes. In the early 20th century it was restored and returned to the Church.

Continue along the road towards Balsall Common. After a short distance turn left on Kixley Lane, which leads to the former Kixley Wharf on the Grand Union Canal. Cross the canal then continue forward to join a footpath across a field to Elvers Green Lane. Turn left along this quiet, winding lane, which eventually takes you across the River Blythe and then to a junction with Hob Lane.

Turn right, and walk to Piercil End to find a footpath which bears right across pasture to a bridge spanning the River Blythe. Once

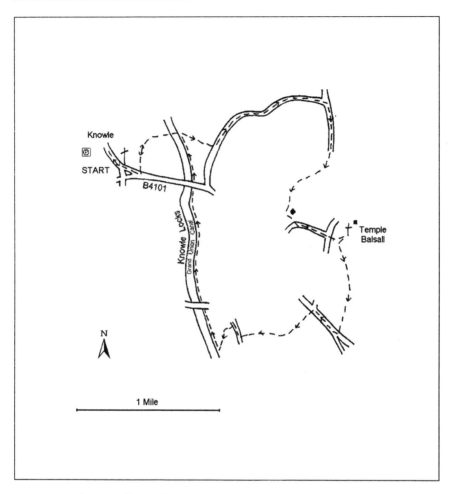

across go diagonally right to a gate giving access to a copse. A clear path leads through the trees to emerge near Springfield House School. Turn right to follow the waymarked route around the perimeter of the school, emerging on the driveway. Turn right for a short distance, until a footpath crosses the drive. Turn left here to Kenilworth Road.

Turn left to a T-junction and then right on to Temple Lane. Almost immediately, join a footpath which leads through woodland. Very soon another footpath is met on the right, and this is our onward route. First, however, it's worth the short detour to the small group of buildings visible ahead at Temple Balsall. This is a tiny community which has developed from an estate of the Knights Templar, an order of warrior monks founded in 1118 to protect pilgrims in the Holy Land. Their work was largely financed by gifts from the aristocracy, which often took the form of land. This was the case at Balsall, which was given by Roger de Mowbray, probably in 1146. A thriving farm was established, and in the 13th century the Old Hall was built, as was St Mary's Church, replacing an earlier chapel.

The Templars did not always live up to their high ideals and, in any case, their increasing wealth inevitably led to envy. In 1308 the order was disbanded and its estates given to a similar organisation, the Knights Hospitaller. Little is known about the Hospitallers at Temple Balsall, but from 1470 the property was leased to a succession of lay tenants until seized by Henry VIII at the Dissolution of the Monasteries. In later years it passed to Elizabeth I's favourite, Robert Dudley, and then to his granddaughters, Lady Anne Holbourne and Lady Katherine Leveson.

The Templars' church had fallen into ruin but Lady Anne paid for its restoration while Lady Katherine endowed a hospital (almshouse) for 20 poor women and a free school for 20 poor boys. The minister of the church was also to serve as schoolteacher and master of the hospital, and a house was provided for him. Lady Katherine set up a board of trustees and their successors still administer the charity today.

The hospital buildings face each other across a courtyard, with the master's house forming the third side of the group. The ladies used to walk each day along the footpath to the Old Hall to collect their bread ration from the bailiff, and the path is still known as the Breadwalk. By 1736 the Old Hall was in a poor state of repair and was replaced by Temple House, which stands opposite the church. Later, the remains of the Old Hall were turned into cottages for the sexton and the curate, and these still stand next to the church.

St Mary's was restored by Sir George Gilbert Scott in 1864 and the schoolroom was replaced around the same time. The hospital has recently been refurbished to provide modern flats and is now open to men as well as women. Returning to the footpath noted earlier, follow it to a junction then turn right. Continue to Green Lane and turn right, then immediately right again at the junction with Chadwick Lane. Turn left when you reach Park Corner, joining a footpath which passes close to a house then continues by field edges to reach a road by Dial House, a lovely, timber-framed building with a sundial adorning its chimney stack.

Turn right beside the road then cross to Heronfield, where another footpath is joined. After passing houses to enter a field, turn right along two sides of the field then continue on a tree-lined path to a pub, where you turn left then go through the car park for access to the towpath of the Grand Union Canal. Turn right, eventually passing Knowle Locks, an impressive flight of five wide locks built in 1932 to replace six narrow ones, the remains of which can still be seen. At Kixley Wharf join the lane to return to Knowle.

Walk 19: Earlswood

Start/finish: Earlswood Station, grid reference 097743.

Summary: Open water is rare in Warwickshire, so the lakes explored in the course of this short and thoroughly undemanding circular walk make for an unexpected treat. Though popular with local walkers, boaters and anglers, they are still relatively rich in wildlife, with spectacular birds such as herons, mute swans and great crested grebes all easily seen.

Length: 5½ miles/8.8km.

Maps: OS Landranger 139, OS Pathfinder 954.

Buses/Coaches: Hardings 186 Portway to Redditch via Earlswood, Fridays.

Trains: Central Trains Stratford to Worcester via Earlswood, daily (on Sundays use The Lakes Station instead).

Parking: Roadside car parking near Earlswood Station, public car park at the recreation ground between the lakes at grid reference 110739.

The Tea Shop

Wellington's Tea Rooms and Restaurant, Manor Farm Craft Centre, Wood Lane, Earlswood, Solihull.

Manor Farm has been in the Osborne family for the last century, but the pressures on modern farming have led to diversification, with redundant farm buildings now housing craft businesses, an ice cream shop and a tea room. Wellington's is a pleasant, heavily beamed room with colourful furnishings, attractive paintings displayed on the brick walls and bundles of dried hops suspended from the beams. With fresh flowers on the tables and friendly service, this is a welcoming place for a break, and there's a good range of hot and cold drinks, snacks and meals, along with a selection of sandwiches, scones and cakes to choose from. Vegetarians should find something suitable but should ask for details. Dogs are welcome and an area is set aside for smokers.

Open: 9.30am-4.30pm daily in summer; Thursday to Sunday only during winter. Telephone: 01564 702570.

The Walk

Earlswood was formerly part of a densely wooded area of the Forest of Arden, which belonged to the Earls of Warwick. Only small areas of woodland survive today, two of which, Clowes Wood and New Fallings Coppice, are explored in this walk. The two are contiguous (a stream runs along the boundary), but Clowes Wood is owned by Warwickshire Wildlife Trust, and New Fallings Coppice by the Bournville Village Trust, though both are managed as nature reserves. They are part of a larger Site of Special Scientific Interest which also includes Earlswood Lakes.

Leaving the station, follow Station Drive to Rumbush Lane and turn right, soon reaching a footpath sign. The well-trodden path leads directly across fields to a stile giving access to Clowes Wood, where you turn right. The wood has a varied flora and fauna, but is basically an acidic woodland with oak, birch, rowan, holly and alder. It also includes other habitats, such as heathland (rare in Warwickshire), wetland and a meadow.

When you reach a glade, bear right and you'll soon come to a railway bridge. Don't cross it but turn left, with the railway just to your right. When the path forks go to the left, following yellow-topped posts, crossing an area of heathland. Then go through more wood-

Engine Pool at Earlswood Lakes

land to reach a cross-paths by a wire fence. Go forward over a footbridge, still following the posts, and keep straight on at all junctions. When you reach a pair of footbridges cross them both. Turn right, with the most westerly of the Earlswood Lakes, Terry's Pool, on your left.

Earlswood Lakes are actually three reservoirs created to provide a water supply for the Stratford Canal. After the lakes were established in the 1820s, Earlswood became a favoured destination for bank holiday outings from Birmingham, with horse-drawn carriages conveying people until the railway was built. Still popular today, they provide a home for many water birds, including herons, grebes, moorhens, coots, mallards, mute swans and Canada geese.

At a junction swing left, passing through an open gateway and following the tree-lined path around the southern edge of the lake. When you reach a dam which divides Terry's Pool from Engine Pool, turn right to walk along the right-hand edge of a recreation ground to a residential street. Turn right, and when you reach number 94, cross to a footpath which leads to Windmill Pool. Go through a gate and turn right beside the pool, then left at the corner to walk along the eastern edge of it.

On reaching a road turn right, then shortly left on to Shutt Lane. At the junction with Salter Street turn left. Surprisingly perhaps, Salter Street is not an old saltway, but is named after a John Salter who, in the 1720s, was living at a farmhouse that later came to be called Salter Street Farm. The parish of Salter Street was created after his death and named after him.

When you reach the Stratford Canal, join the towpath and go straight ahead (that is, heading away from Salter Street Church). At bridge 16 go up to Lady Lane and turn left, passing Earlswood Motor Yacht Club. The lane leads to a crossroads, with Wood Lane opposite. Manor Farm is just a little way down here, but for a more enjoyable route turn left on Norton Lane, towards the engine house which pumps water to the canal. It originally housed a beam engine, but this has long since been replaced by electric pumps. Until 1936 narrowboats carried coal up the feeder to the engine house. Across the road you can see the canal feeder channel.

Turn right by the engine house to walk alongside Engine Pool. When you see a footbridge and path on the right, go this way to reach Wood Lane – Manor Farm is a little to the right. Return the same way to Engine Pool and resume your walk along its edge. When the path

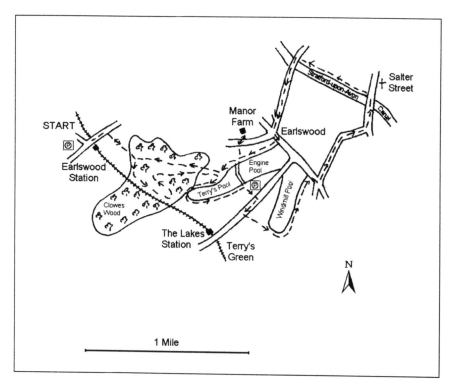

divides, fork right (the path on the left crosses the dam which divides Engine Pool from Terry's Pool) and continue to the point at which you met Terry's Pool near the start of the walk. Go to the right here, into New Fallings Coppice, fork right again and follow a waymarked footpath which leads into grassland. Keep left along its edge until a stile gives access to the wood again. Turn left and descend to a footbridge, then straight on, soon rejoining the route defined by yellow-topped posts. This takes you back to the railway bridge, from where you can retrace your steps along the edge of the wood to the footpath which leads back to Rumbush Lane. Alternatively, and unofficially, a right turn from the bridge takes you directly back to the station on a path used by locals, but not a right of way.

Walk 20: Shipston-on-Stour

Start/finish: High Street, Shipston-on-Stour; grid reference 258406.

Summary: An enjoyable circular walk which takes you over the lower slopes of Brailes Hill, a prominent local landmark. Though there is no access to the top of the hill, there is still some fine walking to be had, particularly on the return leg, which provides good views towards the Cotswolds. There are about 20 stiles and you may also have to climb over a few locked gates.

Length: 8 miles/13km.

Maps: OS Landranger 151, OS Pathfinders 1021 and 1044, OS Outdoor Leisure 45 (shows most of route).

Buses/Coaches: Stagecoach Midland Red X50 Birmingham to Oxford via Shipston, daily; 23 Stratford to Brailes via Shipston, Monday to Saturday; Barry's Coaches Moreton-in-Marsh to Stratford via Shipston, Wednesdays and Fridays; Shipston Link circulars to/from nearby villages.

Trains: Nearest station is Stratford.

Parking: Public car parks in Shipston.

The Tea Shop

Meg Rivers Cake Shop and Traditional English Tea Room, 23A High Street, Shipston-on-Stour.

Tucked away at the junction of High Street and Sheep Street, this little tea room with its quiet, relaxed and friendly atmosphere provides an opportunity to enjoy some of the cakes, biscuits and scones made at the famous Meg Rivers Bakery in Middle Tysoe. An attractive period building inside and out, the tea room makes good use of the classic combination of wooden furnishings and fittings with starched white table linen and blue and white china. The menu includes all the traditional favourites, such as sandwiches, scones and a truly devastating range of fruit cakes, as well as a selection of light lunch dishes, including quiches, savoury flans, salads and soups. The emphasis is on the use of organic ingredients and local free-range eggs. All the cakes and biscuits are suitable for vegetarians and there is a good selection of vegetarian soups, but vegetarian cheese is not used. You can buy cakes, biscuits and preserves to take away, with most of the cakes featured in the Meg Rivers Mail Order Cata-

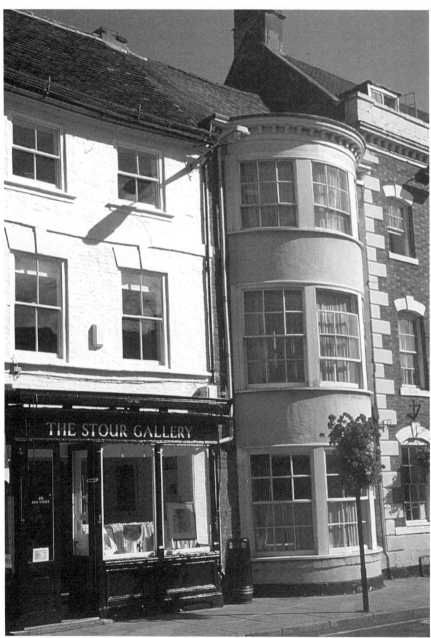

Shipston-on-Stour

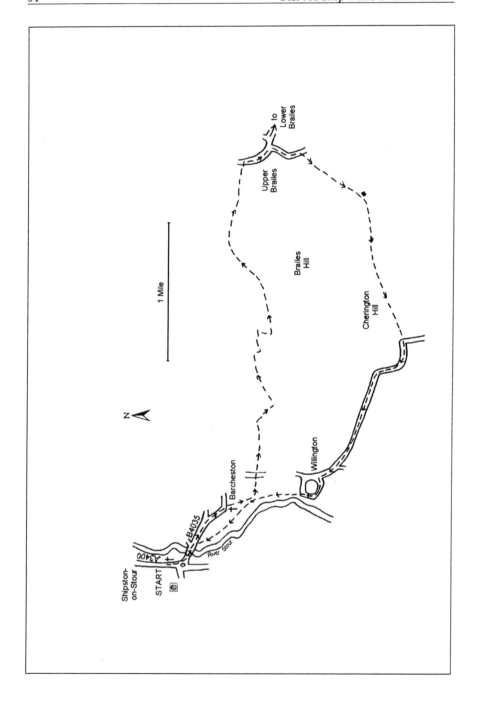

logue available (you may have seen it advertised in the classified sections of the Sunday broadsheets). Books and crayons are provided to keep children happy, and on summer Sunday afternoons a young musician entertains older visitors. There is some outside seating and smokers are welcome to use this. Dogs, too, are welcome outside.

Open: 10.00am-5.00pm Monday-Saturday; 12.00am-5.00pm Sundays and Bank Holiday Mondays. Telephone: 01608 662217.

The Walk

Shipston was for centuries a major sheep market and commercial centre for the rich, agricultural area of south Warwickshire known as The Feldon, though it was actually part of Worcestershire until 1931. Beautiful houses from the 17th, 18th and 19th centuries bear witness to its past prosperity, based not only on its status as a market town, but also on its position astride a busy coaching route. A couple of old coaching inns still grace its streets today.

Walk through the marketplace to the main road, near St Edmund's Church, and turn right. At a junction turn left on the B4035 to Brailes and Banbury. Take care crossing a bridge over the Stour as there's no footway. Once across there's a footway on the left. Ignore the turn for Honington and keep straight on, also ignoring a footpath on the right.

Join an unsigned lane on the right which leads to the tiny hamlet of Barcheston, which has a 17th-century manor house, rectory and church. The latter is a lovely building with a 14th-century tower and, reportedly, an interesting interior, though it is kept locked. A key may be obtained at the Old Rectory.

Leave the church by the lych-gate and go forward over a green towards a stile ahead. This gives access to a large arable field and you should walk straight ahead, close to its right-hand edge. At a stile, don't cross but turn left by the field edge to reach a lane. Cross and continue opposite by the right-hand field edge. At a waymarked post, cross to the other side of the hedge and continue in the same direction, towards Brailes Hill, a notable landmark visible from much of the north-east Cotswolds and instantly recognisable by the clump of trees which crowns it.

Turn right at the edge of the field, taking care on uneven ground, before going over a stile and continuing in the same direction along the edge of pasture. You soon come to a gate on the left where two footpaths are signposted. Take the left-hand one, which runs along the field edge. As you pass to the right of a barn you'll have to climb a couple of tied-up gates to reach a stile. Go forward across cattle pasture, and at the far side join a green lane which brings you into a large arable field. Turn right along its edge for about 200 metres, on a bridleway, to a waymarked post, where you turn left. At the top of the field, below a belt of scrub-covered rough pasture, the bridleway turns left again, past oak trees and gorse. Climb to a gate, go through and turn left once more, enjoying fine views of seemingly endless fields and hedges, punctuated at intervals by church spires.

At a junction join a footpath and go uphill through woodland, up a flight of steps and across an arable field to a stile where two paths are signed. Take the left-hand one, which crosses a field, descends through a dingle, crosses another field then passes through the garden of a cottage. Continue past more houses into Upper Brailes and turn right.

Upper and Lower Brailes together make up a substantial village which was, in medieval times, an important market town with a castle, the earthworks of which are still visible. It was the third largest town in Warwickshire, after Warwick and Coventry. The church, at Lower Brailes, has a fine Perpendicular tower, and is known as the Cathedral of the Feldon, its sheer size reminding visitors of the past importance of Brailes. This walk passes through Upper Brailes only, but it's not far to Lower Brailes and it's a worthwhile detour.

Turn right when you come to Henbrook Lane and stay on the lane until you can join a bridleway on the right. After passing a house it becomes a deep holloway, also a stream-bed at times, before eventually emerging into sheep pasture. Go straight on across the field close to the right-hand edge, enjoying wide open views as you start to contour around the side of Brailes Hill. Passing a farm, the bridleway makes a right turn, and runs alongside the left-hand edge of the field then through a bridle gate next to some pine trees. Immediately turn right through another gate and then left to continue in the same direction as before, crossing pasture grazed by sheep and Jersey cattle. Keep going across fields in the same direction, as the bridleway gradually descends Cherington Hill towards the Stour Valley. Go diagonally left down the final field to arrive at a gated road. Turn left then immediately right, and walk along the lane into Willington.

Take the second turning on the left, opposite a large, brick, modern house. Ignore a footpath by Rushway House and turn right, then left at the next junction, joining a footpath.

When you reach a footbridge, don't cross the Stour but go through a gate ahead and follow the path running to the right of the river, which takes you back to Barcheston. Turn left on a "no through road" and pass The Manor to join another footpath. After a few paces go over a stile into a field and walk to another stile visible ahead in the far hedge. Keep forward on what is now an obvious route. It leads to the road, where you turn left into Shipston.

Walk 21: Ebrington Hill

Start/finish: Mickleton, grid reference 161435.

Summary: An undulating circular walk in the Cotswolds which makes use of well-defined paths through pasture, arable and woodland. It may be cheating a little as it's partly in Gloucestershire, but it does take you to Warwickshire's highest point and (arguably) Warwickshire's loveliest village. Other highlights include gardens at Kiftsgate Court and Hidcote Manor (but try to avoid summer Sundays and Bank Holiday Mondays if you plan to visit Hidcote).

Length: 9 miles/14.5km.

Maps: OS Landranger 151, OS Pathfinders 1020 and 1021.

Buses/Coaches: Stagecoach Midland Red 21 Stratford to Bourton-on-the-Water via Mickleton, daily; 22 Stratford to Broadway via Mickleton, Monday to Saturday; Castleways Coaches 569 (Cotswold Explorer) Moreton-in-Marsh to Broadway/Evesham via Mickleton and Hidcote, daily; Barry's Coaches Moreton to Stratford via Ilmington, Wednesdays and Fridays; Shipston Link Shipston circular via Ilmington, Thursdays; Stagecoach Stroud Valleys X48 Stroud to Coventry via Mickleton, Wednesdays and Sundays in July and August; Cresswells 600 Chipping Campden to Evesham via Mickleton, Fridays; 608 Chipping Campden to Cheltenham via Mickleton, Thursdays and Saturdays.

Trains: Nearest station is Honeybourne, but Castleways 569 is timed to provide connections with trains at Moreton (and some at Evesham).

Parking: Some roadside spaces available in Mickleton. Alternatively, some parking is available at the top of Ebrington Hill. There is a National Trust car park at Hidcote but it is only for those visiting the garden.

The Tea Shop
The Thatched Tea Bar, Hidcote Manor Garden.

The National Trust has two refreshment areas at Hidcote, but it is this one which is more likely to appeal to walkers. Light refreshments are served from a stone and thatch barn which opens onto a walled courtyard adjacent to a plant sales centre. The tea bar is pleasant and sheltered, but please note that it is very much an alfresco setting. Anybody requiring indoor seating should try the Garden Restaurant, which offers morning coffee, afternoon tea and a full lunch menu, all with waitress service. However, it's rather smart for the average muddy-booted walker. The Tea Bar serves a perfectly adequate range of drinks, cakes, scones and ice creams, some of which are suitable for vegetarians. Despite the outdoor setting, dogs are not permitted.

Open: 10.30am-5.45pm daily except Tuesday and Friday, April to end of September (open Tuesdays in June and July) but times may vary according to the weather. (Times quoted are for the Tea Bar; the Garden Restaurant has slightly different hours and a longer season.) Telephone: 01386 438703.

Note: Hidcote Manor Garden is a National Trust property, and while the Thatched Tea Bar is freely open to everyone, entry to the Garden Restaurant requires payment of the entrance fee or production of a membership card.

Hidcote Bartrim

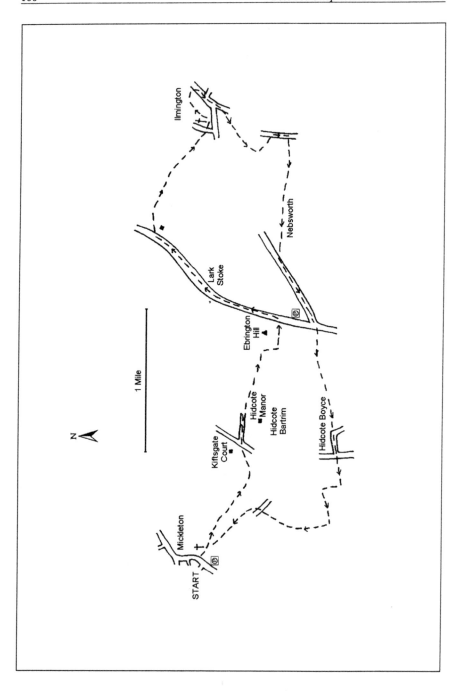

The Walk

Often regarded as the northernmost Cotswold village, Mickleton is not particularly memorable in itself, but it has an attractive situation beneath the hills and is a good starting point for walks. Begin in the centre of the village, joining a "no through road" near a phone box. Pass The Manor and the church to join the Heart of England Way, which goes forward into a field. Go diagonally right to the far corner, through a gate and straight on by field edges until you enter a large sloping pasture. Follow a well-trodden path which climbs gently, veering slightly left. On the left, surrounded by fine trees, is Kiftsgate Court, whose celebrated garden, created after World War One by Heather Muir, is open to the public.

Keep climbing, aiming for a blue gate a little to the right of the entrance gates to Kiftsgate. Join a lane at a junction and go straight ahead to the car park for Hidcote Manor Garden. The onward route is straight on along a clear track, but first you may wish to visit Hidcote – turn right if you do. You'll come first to the Tea Bar and then to the garden entrance.

Hidcote Manor Garden was acquired by Gertrude Winthrop in 1907, and over the next 40 years her son, Major Lawrence Johnston, transformed it into one of the most influential of 20th-century gardens. It is designed as a series of small gardens, separated by walls and hedges, each with its own atmosphere. Major Johnston gave the garden to the National Trust in 1948. Just a short stroll away is Hidcote Bartrim, a cluster of lovely cottages, several of them thatched.

Resuming the walk, return to the track noted earlier and follow it uphill, enjoying good views of Broadway Hill, Bredon Hill and the Malverns. The track eventually makes a sharp right turn, and then a sharp left, heading for three TV masts crowning Ebrington Hill, the highest point in Warwickshire (850ft/261 m), but only just, as the trig point stands on the Gloucestershire border. Pass close by the masts and on to a lane, a former drove road.

Turn left, walking into a superb view of Warwickshire as the lane descends to Lower Lark Stoke. On reaching the entrance to a house, join the Centenary Way. Pass to the left of the entrance gates, down an arable field and on towards a stile roughly halfway between two telegraph poles. Enter a pasture and bear right up a slope, more or less parallel with a brook below.

Soon with a hedge on your left, continue to another stile, climb over and turn right along the edges of fields. Ilmington comes into view now and there's another stile on the right. The path forks here but stay on the Centenary Way, which crosses the stile then goes diagonally down the field. There are also green and white waymarkers here, indicating a Countryside Stewardship site.

Go down the field towards a group of willows, then climb to the far top corner, where there are two stiles. The first gives access to another Countryside Stewardship site, limestone grassland which supports a variety of wild flowers. Go over the second stile and diagonally left on the Centenary Way to the far corner of a large, rolling pasture. At the next stile the Centenary Way turns to the right – leave it here and go to the left, down towards Ilmington.

Reaching a cluster of buildings, take a left turn through a stable yard and down a path which brings you out opposite the 11th-century church of St Mary the Virgin, with its square tower and superb Norman doorway. Over the porch can be seen the coat of arms of Simon de Montfort, once patron of the church. The interior contains some fine memorials to local families and modern woodwork made in the 1930s by Robert Thompson of Kilburn, whose signature of a carved mouse occurs 11 times.

Walk along a lime avenue which skirts the churchyard. At the far side, by a cottage, turn left and soon right, passing between a pond and a house called Bevingtons. Turn left on another path which runs along the backs of some fine stone houses. When you come to a passageway on the right, take this to join the main street and turn right, admiring what is probably the nearest Warwickshire has to a truly Cotswold village. Sheltered by Ilmington Downs, its gracious buildings are a mixture of warm stone and mellow brick, with stone, tile and thatch roofs. Its name recalls the elms which once grew freely here, before Dutch elm disease took its toll.

Go straight on to the village green and fork left, passing to the left of the war memorial. Keep straight on along a "no through road" known as Grump Street, and past Crab Mill, one of the oldest houses in the village, dating from 1711. Its name refers to crab apples, not eight-legged crustaceans.

After Primrose Bank, the road continues as a hedged track known as Tinker's Lane. Ignore all branching footpaths, continuing to the end of the track. Go forward into a field as far as a drinking trough then turn left on a fairly well-trodden path which climbs a slope to a stile in the hedge at the top. Cross another field to a lane and turn right, climbing gently to meet a cross-track where you turn right again on a hedged bridleway, Pig Lane. It climbs gently, providing marvellous views, before levelling out. Continue towards two masts ahead, with Warwickshire on your right, the bosky Gloucestershire wolds on your left.

The track descends to meet a road, where you turn left to walk up Ebrington Hill. When you reach the old drove road again, go through a gate to a footpath. The well-defined route runs straight ahead to the left of a wall at first, then diagonally left across hummocky pasture to join a farm track. This descends to Hidcote Boyce, a lovely hamlet with a sloping street bordered by flower-filled cottage gardens.

Keep straight on to a T-junction and join a footpath almost directly opposite. When you reach the end of an orchard and kitchen garden, turn right then soon left, descending a field then crossing a brook. Walk up the edge of the next field and then follow a track which passes to the right of a barn. Turn right on the Heart of England Way and follow it to the road, crossing to a footpath opposite. Enter a pasture and go through a gate on the left then head towards Mickleton Church, with a hedge on your right. After going through a gate in the far right-hand corner of the field, the path continues through woodland and on along the edge of pasture to Mickleton.

Walk 22: The Rollrights

Start/finish: Long Compton, grid reference 287326.

Summary: Fine countryside, an interesting village and intriguing ancient monuments
                      feature in this circular walk. Though the terrain is undulating, it is relatively
                      gentle and the paths are well-defined. There is only one stile but you may
                      have to climb over a padlocked gate.

Length: 7 miles/11.2km.

Maps: OS Landranger 151, OS Pathfinder 1044, OS Outdoor Leisure 45 shows
                      part of the route.

Buses/Coaches: Stagecoach Midland Red X50 Birmingham to Oxford via Long Compton,
                      daily; 487/488 Banbury to Chipping Norton via Great Rollright, Monday to
                      Saturday; 77 Moreton to Banbury via Long Compton, Thursdays and Sat-
                      urdays; Barry's Coaches Moreton to Stratford via Long Compton, school-
                      days; Shipston Link from Shipston, Wednesdays and Fridays; National
                      Express 511 Great Malvern to London calls at nearby Chipping Norton
                      daily (connections by bus or taxi).

Trains: Nearest station is Kingham.

Parking: Lay-by at junction of A3400 with a minor road at the south end of Long
                      Compton, grid reference 290320. Alternatively, you may be able to
                      park at Hill Barn Farm, but should confirm this with the staff in the tea
                      shop first.

The Tea Shop
Hill Barn Farm, Great Rollright, Chipping Norton.

Owned and run by the Wyatt family, this spacious restaurant, with
fresh flowers on all the tables, and paintings by local artists on the
walls, makes a very pleasant place for a break. There are far-reaching
views to be enjoyed too, especially if you make use of the outdoor
seating. Children are welcome, as are guide dogs, but other dogs are
permitted outside only. All food is home-cooked on the premises
and includes cakes, pastries, scones, and a range of hot dishes such
as pasta, grills, jackets, quiche and fish. There are plenty of vegetarian options and all soups are made with vegetable stock. The wide
range of drinks includes many herbal and fruit teas. Adjoining the
tea room are a superbly stocked farm shop and garden centre.

Open: 10.00am-6.00pm May to September; 10.00am-5.00pm October to April. Telephone: 01608 684835.

The Walk

Long Compton was once notorious for its witches, but today it's plagued by traffic instead. Nevertheless, it's an attractive village of stone-built houses accompanied by a fine church with a two-storeyed, thatched lych-gate. No one knows what its original purpose was, but it has been suggested that it was once a cottage whose lower storey has been removed.

Though Long Compton is basically a linear village, there are several side streets which are worth exploring before walking north through the village. At the top end, between Victoria Cottage and a road junction, turn right on a footpath, soon bearing left towards a metal gate. Cross a field to another and continue along a track. This is undulating terrain, comprising mixed farmland with plenty of trees, and the route is part of the Macmillan Way.

Entering a plantation, Long Compton Woods, turn round for a good retrospective view, with the church set against an attractive, hilly backdrop. Continuing the walk, climb to a T-junction and turn right. The path quite soon emerges from the trees and continues along the edge of Whichford Wood.

Turn right when you reach a bridleway running at right angles to the footpath, beside a hedge. The bridleway descends and is clearly waymarked. When you come to a junction with a footpath turn left, still on the bridleway. After crossing a brook the bridleway soon turns left by a hedge. Though no longer waymarked, the route remains obvious. As you approach a wood, make a right turn and then a left, following waymarks once again. In the final field bear right as you approach the road and then turn right.

As you walk along the road you can look down on Long Compton and most of the route you've just walked. You'll soon come to Hill Barn Farm and can take a well-earned refreshment break. When you leave the farm, turn left along the road, retracing your steps for a short distance to a road junction, where you turn right. After about 300 metres, join a footpath on the right, climbing over a padlocked gate. The path begins as a hedged green track before becoming a field-edge path and finally a cross-field one, but the route is never in doubt. Climb a stile at the far side to join a road and turn right, then left, to walk along the main road, an ancient ridgeway route running along a windswept Cotswold spur at 700ft(216m). The road now forms the border between Warwickshire and Oxfordshire and offers wide views over both. The ridgeway is believed to have been part of one of Britain's earliest and most important tracks, the so-called Jurassic Way along the limestone belt from the shores of the Humber to the Dorset coast.

Before long you'll reach the Rollright Stones, three separate prehistoric monuments. First to be seen are the Whispering Knights on the left, then the King Stone on the right and finally the King's Men on the left.

Nobody really knows what these stones represent, or even how old they are, but the general consensus is that the Whispering Knights, actually four uprights and a fallen capstone, are the remains of a burial chamber constructed in the Neolithic period, maybe 4000 years ago. The King's Men, a circle of around 70 weather-worn uprights, and the King Stone, a solitary, intriguingly shaped stone taller than a man, are most likely Bronze Age, at least 3000 years old, and probably erected for ritual purposes.

The Rollrights seem to have always enjoyed considerable mystical significance, and in the Middle Ages peasants would chip pieces off to keep as charms against the Devil. Witches are reputed to have gathered here in Tudor times, and until comparatively recently local people used to meet at the stones once a year for dancing and drinking, perhaps continuing a long tradition of fertility rites. Today, battered and broken, the stones still cast a spell and New Age mystics dowse for ley lines and talk of fair-

The King Stone, The Rollrights

ies dancing round the King Stone while strange sounds emanate from the Whispering Knights at a full moon.

Legends which seek to explain the Rollrights are plentiful, but the best known concerns an ambitious king and his army, confronted here by a witch, Mother Shipton, who shrieked at the king:

> *Seven long strides thou shalt take*
> *And if Long Compton thou canst see*
> *King of England thou shalt be.*

As the king strode confidently forward to view Long Compton,

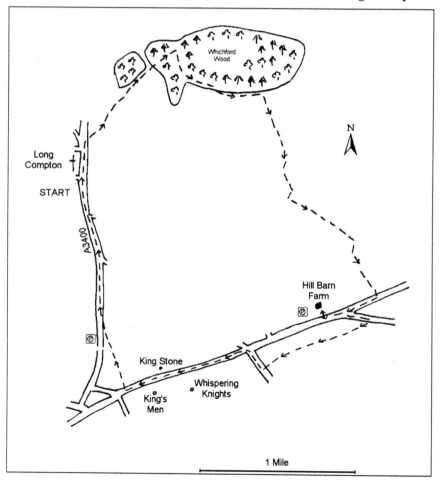

which he knew to be below the ridge, he found it obscured by a mound, and the witch cried:

As Long Compton thou canst not see
King of England thou shalt not be.
Rise up stick and stand still stone,
For King of England thou shalt be none.
Thou and thy men hoar stones shall be
And I myself an eldern tree.

The king was turned into the King Stone and his loyal men became the stone circle, while a treacherous group, busy plotting his downfall, became the Whispering Knights. In an Arthurian twist to the legend, it is claimed that there is a great cave beneath the King Stone in which he keeps watch. In England's hour of need the spell will be broken, and he and his men will hasten forth to defend their country.

Having inspected the stones, continue to a crossroads and join a footpath on the right. As you enter a field there is a superb view of Warwickshire and Gloucestershire laid out in front of you. Walk forward to meet a hedge and then keep left of it as you descend towards Long Compton in the valley below. On reaching a road turn right and walk to the village, taking great care as traffic here is both faster and more frequent than you might expect.

𝒲𝒶𝓁𝓀 23: Edgehill

Start/finish: Sun Rising Hill, near Upton House; grid reference 363458.

Summary: A thoroughly delightful circular walk on gently undulating terrain, which includes two of Warwickshire's loveliest villages and the long, tree-clad escarpment of Edgehill, on which Charles I unfurled his standard in 1642 before the first major battle of the Civil War. The opportunity may also be taken to visit the National Trust's splendid Upton House.

Length: 5½ miles/8.8km.

Maps: OS Landranger 151, OS Pathfinder 1021.

Buses/Coaches: Stagecoach Midland Red X70/270 Stratford to Banbury via Sun Rising Hill and Upton House, Monday to Saturday; 210 Banbury to Stratford via Edgehill, Radway and Ratley, schooldays; 502 Kineton to Banbury via Radway and Ratley, Thursdays and Saturdays.

Trains: Nearest station is Banbury.

Parking: Lay-by at Sun Rising Hill; alternatively you may use the National Trust car park when Upton House is open (assuming you intend to visit the house).

The Tea Shop
Upton House, near Banbury.

Not one, but two gleaming white Agas provide a focal point in this former kitchen, where old wooden units, colourful tablecloths and fresh flowers offset the rather clinical white-tiled walls. There is seating for about three dozen people, but a pleasant sense of spaciousness is retained in this high-ceilinged room. Service is friendly and two high chairs are thoughtfully provided for small children. Choose from a range of set teas or from the superb variety of individual cakes, scones and teabreads on offer, or sample the special Upton shortbread. The scones and some of the cakes are suitable for vegetarians. The choice of drinks is good, including fruit teas and elderflower cordial. Ice creams are also available.

Open: 2.00pm-6.00pm Saturday to Wednesday, April to October (last teas at 5.30pm on weekdays in April and October). Telephone: 01295 670266.

Note: Upton House is a National Trust property so an entrance fee is payable, except by Trust members, even if you intend only to visit the tea room. Dogs are not permitted within the grounds.

The Walk

The steep slope by which the A422 climbs Edgehill is known as Sun Rising Hill, and there's a lay-by here which makes a suitable parking place for those arriving by car. If you travel by bus you can also start here, or alternatively you can ask the driver to drop you at the entrance to Upton House, starting the walk there instead.

Assuming you begin at Sun Rising Hill, head west (downhill) for a few paces to where the road is crossed by a footpath which forms part of both the Centenary Way and the Macmillan Way. Turn right on it as it heads through the woodland of Edgehill Covert. The path initially swings left, then right. There should be a boundary wall on your left, with some fine beech trees beside it and a very large ash tree. The path then continues through newly planted woodland to merge with another path coming from the left. Continue in the same direction, with fields visible through the trees on your right, and a steep wooded slope falling away on your left.

Eventually pass Edgehill Farm and emerge on a lane. Turn left for a short distance until you see the path signposted on the right. It makes the short climb to the top of Edgehill and then continues along the woodland edge until reaching a T-junction with another track. Go left here to an area of beautiful old beech trees. Very soon the path forks; stay on the left-hand track, a holloway (King John's Lane) which descends between overhanging trees.

Soon after leaving the trees, turn right when you see a waymarked post. The path runs straight across two fields, passes between a small, brick barn and a pond and then bears left to a concealed stile which leads into a paddock. Follow its edge, and then go straight on into Radway, a charming village built of local Hornton stone.

Turn left along the lane, passing several lovely houses, including Radway Grange, an Elizabethan mansion in fine grounds. It was inherited by Gothic Revival architect Sanderson Miller in 1735. His friends, who visited him at Radway, included Pitt the Elder, Lord North, Horace Walpole and Henry Fielding, who is said to have written part of *Tom Jones* here.

At the main road turn right, though you may first wish to visit the church opposite. This was rebuilt in 1866 in a new position, and contains a monument to Sanderson Miller, who died in 1780, and another to Captain Kingsmill, a Royalist officer killed at Edgehill.

More lovely houses line the road, many of them thatched. Join a

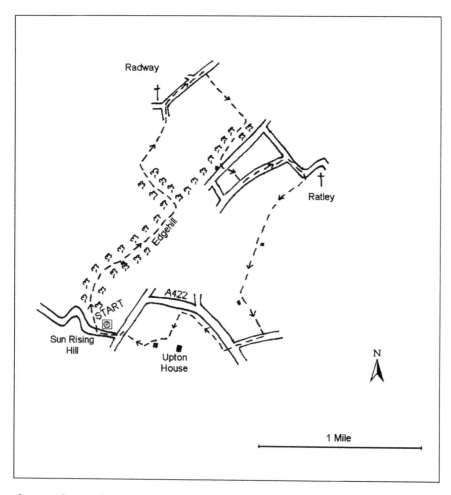

footpath on the right by Grafton Cottage. It leads between gardens and orchards to pastureland. Go straight ahead, climbing towards the trees topping Edgehill.

In October 1642 Royalist troops under Charles I and Prince Rupert gathered at the top of the hill before charging down to the plain below to engage the Parliamentarians, led by the Earl of Essex, in the first real battle of the English Civil War. The outcome was inconclusive but it resulted in the death of around 4000 men. After the battle Essex's forces withdrew to Kineton and Charles spent the night in King's Leys Barn before breakfasting at Radway. Neither was keen to reopen battle and Charles continued his march to Oxford while Essex withdrew to Warwick. The actual battle site is now in the hands of the Ministry of Defence and there is no public access.

The view from the upper slopes of Edgehill includes the Vale of the Red Horse, so-called because a horse was cut into the turf on the slopes above Tysoe in Saxon times. It was ploughed up around 1800.

Go forward into Castle Wood and turn right, now back on the Centenary Way. There are some magnificent trees here, planted by Sanderson Miller in the 18th century. When you come to a junction, fork left on a bridleway which climbs to the Castle Inn, which has a tower by Sanderson Miller, modelled on Guy's Tower at Warwick Castle. It was sited to mark the spot where the Royal standard was raised before the battle.

The Castle Inn

Cross the road to a footpath by Cavalier Cottage and follow it to a lane, turning left towards Ratley. Turn right down the High Street, which is lined by attractive Hornton stone cottages. When the lane bends left your ongoing footpath is on the right, but first you might like to see the rest of the village. There's a church in Hornton stone, dating from about 1250, and the remains of a preaching cross of about the same age. Nearby are some lovely cottages and a splendid farmhouse, and a pub, the Rose and Crown, which claims to have been established in 1098.

Returning to the footpath, walk towards the entrance to Manor Farm. As you reach the gate look for a stile on the right which gives access to a field. Follow the right-hand field edge until it turns a corner. Go straight on instead, down a slope towards a stile. Walk diagonally left up the next field to the far corner, where there are two stiles. Climb the one on the left and go forward along a field edge. Cross another stile and go straight on along the edge of the next field, descending quite steeply into a valley and passing a derelict barn. After going through a gate, the path continues as a farm track across pasture before turning left over a stile and past a barn. Keep going along a tree-lined path, then over a broken stile into a field and straight ahead to a lane. Turn right, then right again at the road to Upton House.

Built of mellow local stone, Upton is impressive and imposing, with a formal façade. The house dates from 1695 and contains an outstanding collection of paintings, tapestries, porcelain, Chelsea figures and 18th-century furniture. The garden is also of great interest, with magnificent herbaceous borders, terraces, a kitchen garden, a water garden and ornamental pools.

Close to the entrance is the access road to Home Farm – cross this to join a footpath at a stile. Go diagonally down a long, narrow field to find a gate near the far corner. Pass through here and through another gate a few paces ahead, and then go diagonally right so that you pass just to the left of a large ash tree and descend a bank towards Home Farm (now the offices of Alliance Medical Limited). Go through a gate and turn right over rough grassland, then step over a low fence and go diagonally left across a car park. Leave it by a gate in the far corner and join a track which bears left across pasture. Pass through a gate where a fence meets a stone wall and follow the wall to the road. Turn left and stay with the road as it bends right to Sun Rising Hill, ignoring a turning to Tysoe.

🎵 *Walk 24: Atherstone*

Start: Long Street, Atherstone; grid reference 308978.

Finish: Atherstone Road, Hartshill Green; grid reference326946.

Summary: The Nuneaton area doesn't automatically spring to mind when deciding
                     where to go for a walk – but cast preconceptions aside and try this enjoy-
                     able linear walk, which includes a canal towpath, woodland, fields and a
                     country park. You're almost certain to be pleasantly surprised and it's a
                     very easy walk too. If you want to make it a circular walk, you can do so by
                     following the canal back to Atherstone (about 3½ miles/5.6km).

Length: 4½ miles/7.2km.

Maps: OS Landranger 140, OS Pathfinder 914.

Buses/Coaches: Stagecoach Midland Red 48/X48 Coventry/Nuneaton to Atherstone via
                     Hartshill Green, Monday to Saturday; 41 Nuneaton to Atherstone and/or
                     Ridge Lane, Monday to Saturday; Arriva Midlands North X76 Birmingham
                     to Nuneaton via Atherstone and Hartshill Green, Monday to Saturday;
                     766 Tamworth to Atherstone, Monday to Friday; De Luxe Coaches 499
                     Baddesley Ensor to Atherstone, Monday to Saturday; Midland Fox 720
                     Tamworth to Hinckley via Atherstone and Hartshill Green, Monday to Fri-
                     day.

Trains: Central Trains Rugby to Stafford (Trent Valley Line) via Atherstone, Mon-
                     day to Saturday, but very few trains actually stop at Atherstone.

Parking: Public car park in town centre.

The Tea Shop

The Old Bakery, 94 Long Street, Atherstone.

The sign outside Mary Martin's popular restaurant still proclaims in
a traditional curly script "Bakers and Confectioners" and the entire
old-fashioned shop front is still intact – if only more like this had
survived. It's traditional in style inside, too, with dark, varnished
woodwork, William Morris-inspired wallpaper and plaster ceiling
roses. A friendly place, it's very popular with locals, many of whom
are regulars. The menu is very comprehensive, with a good range of
home-cooked meals including lasagne, spaghetti Bolognese, vegetarian cannelloni and vegetable crumble. Also available are breakfasts, snacks on toast, salads and chip butties. Portions are generous,

and even simple snacks such as jackets, sandwiches etc. come with a substantial, freshly prepared salad garnish. There's a good selection of scones, cakes, puddings and desserts and hot and cold drinks. A number of items are suitable for vegetarians. Guide dogs are welcome and there are both smoking and non-smoking areas.

Open: 9.00am-3.30pm Monday to Saturday. Telephone: 01827 720050.

Coventry Canal at Atherstone

The Walk

Atherstone is a pleasantly understated sort of place with some elegant Georgian buildings. In the 18th century it was an important coach stop, thanks to its position astride Watling Street, and there are still some former coaching inns on Long Street, which, incidentally, lives up to its name.

After you've explored the town centre, head north on Long Street and near the railway station you'll find Old Watling Street, which takes you under the railway to the Coventry Canal. Turn left along the towpath, passing a few of the 11 locks which constitute the Atherstone Flight. At Outwoods Bridge (38) leave the canal, turning right on a bridleway. Just as you approach a house, turn left on to a footpath which crosses a valley, taking a well-trodden route towards a wood, Purley Park. Turn right along the edge of the wood, before eventually entering it as the path swings left.

Emerging from the trees on Purley Chase Lane, turn right, passing through countryside which is at first a mixture of beautiful woodland and ugly quarries before it settles down into pleasant, agricultural land, mainly pastoral, with plenty of trees and hedges. Though the lane is very quiet, the vehicles which do use it travel too fast, so take care.

At Ridge Lane cross to a footpath almost opposite which leads into a large field. Go straight on along field edges until a stile on the left allows you to join the Centenary Way. Follow the right-hand field edge to Ladywood Farm. Pass to the left of the farm buildings and through a cattle pasture then straight on by a hedge until a stile gives access to a field. Go straight across to join a lane and turn left, then immediately right on an attractive, wooded lane. This leads to Oldbury Cutting Picnic Area, created on the site of a dismantled railway. Enter the site at a bend in the lane and walk straight ahead along the course of the former railway for about 500 metres, until you see a stile on the left. Descend steps and go forward across three fields until forced to turn right. Very soon, a stile and footbridge on the left give access to a narrow field. Cross this then turn left, passing an old quarry and following a fenced path beneath a gorse-covered bank. Walk past Moorwood Rare Breed Farm, which is open daily to the public, and at the next junction turn right past holly hedges. Go over a stile, bear right uphill and follow power lines to a road.

Cross over to enter Hartshill Hayes Country Park, which takes its name from Hugh de Hardreshull, who, in 1125, built a castle in the area now known as Hartshill Green. Only a motte and scant traces of masonry remain today. The park comprises a large expanse of woodland and open grassland on a ridge overlooking the Anker Valley. It offers panoramic views across four counties, and on a clear day the Peak District is visible.

Hugh de Hardreshull was a fairly recent resident for the area was first settled in prehistoric times and the earthworks of an Iron Age hill fort, Oldbury, still survive. During the third century the Romans were active in the locality, and some historians believe that it was at Mancetter, just below the ridge, that they finally defeated the warrior queen Boudicca in AD60.

Just to your right is a large area of woodland, which supports a var-

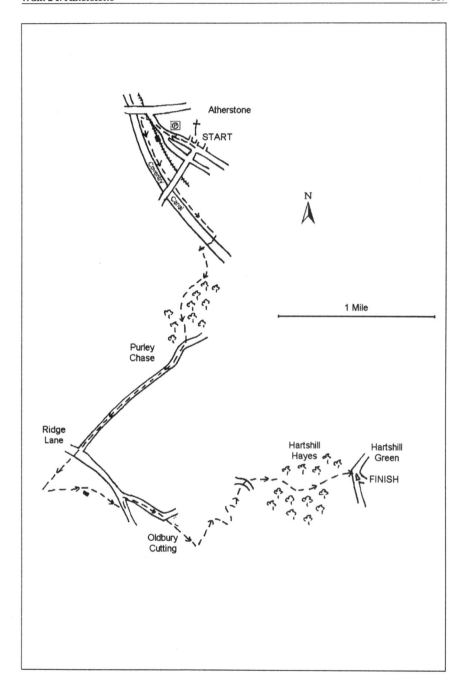

ied bird population – with luck, you may see a sparrowhawk, and you should certainly see jays and woodpeckers, as well as many less spectacular woodland species. Bear right by the woodland edge then right again on a footpath which soon enters the wood. Fork left, pass a picnic table and go left at the next junction. Descend into a valley and at a major T-junction turn left, then right, following yellow way-marks. Descend steps, cross a footbridge, and just keep straight on, ignoring branching paths and soon climbing out of the valley, enjoying excellent views as you leave the trees. A flight of steps takes you to Trentham Road, where you turn right then left to Atherstone Road. If you're treating this as a linear walk you can catch a bus here. If returning on foot to Atherstone, follow the road left to the canal to join the towpath.

Walk 25: Coombe Country Park

Start/finish: New Close Wood, Binley Woods, Coventry; grid reference 404773.

Summary: Right on the edge of Coventry, but you'd never guess. The highlight of this easy circular walk is Coombe Country Park, with its prolific birdlife, but there is also some lovely woodland to enjoy, as well as pleasant farmland.

Length: 8 miles/13km.

Maps: OS Landranger 140, OS Pathfinders 935, 936 and 956.

Buses/Coaches: Stagecoach Midland Red X86/86 Coventry to Rugby via Binley Woods, daily; 207 Rugby to Nuneaton via Brinklow, Wednesdays; A Line Travel 585 Rugby to Coventry via Coombe Abbey, Monday to Saturday.

Trains: Nearest station is Coventry.

Parking: Parking area on the north side of Binley Road (A428), where the Centenary Way enters New Close Wood. Alternatively, you can start the walk at Coombe Abbey, where there is a large pay and display car park.

The Tea Shop

Heron's Table, Coombe Country Park, Brinklow Road, Coventry.

Managed by Eurest on behalf of Coventry City Council, this is a bright, cheerful, modern place with lots of seating and an extensive menu. Choose from meals such as chicken curry or pasta florentine, or from a wide range of snacks such as jacket potatoes, sandwiches, veggie burgers or soup. Baked goods include scones, Danish pastries, and assorted cakes. There are special children's meals, a reasonable choice for vegetarians and a good selection of hot and cold drinks. Dogs are welcome as long as they are well-controlled.

Open: 9.00am-7.00pm daily, April to September; 9.00am-5.00pm daily, October to March (closed Christmas Day). Telephone: 01203 453720.

The Walk

Join the bridleway (the Centenary Way) into New Close Wood, soon forking left on a long, straight track known as Twelve O'Clock Ride, which was once a carriage road to Coombe Abbey. When you emerge

Canada Goose at Coombe Pool

from the wood, just carry straight on, soon crossing a road and continuing forward into Coombe Country Park. You'll soon reach a modern, red-brick building – this is the visitor centre and it's where you'll find the Heron's Table.

Coombe Abbey was founded by Cistercian monks in 1150. They used the surrounding land for rearing sheep and Coombe eventually became the most powerful monastery in Warwickshire. After the Dissolution in 1539 the estate changed hands many times. The abbey was converted into a mansion, and rebuilt more than once, formal gardens were created and sheepwalk was enclosed as parkland. In the 1770s Capability Brown was engaged to redesign the grounds in a less formal style. He created natural-looking woodland and dammed Smite Brook to create Coombe Pool and Top Pool. The estate was broken up in 1922 but acquired piecemeal by Coventry City Council from 1938 onwards. Coombe Abbey itself is now a luxury hotel, but Coombe Country Park is open to the public and attracts over 300 000 visitors a year.

Coombe Pool is the second largest water body in Warwickshire and supports a wealth of wildlife, particularly birds. The county's largest heronry is to be found here, with up to 50 pairs breeding

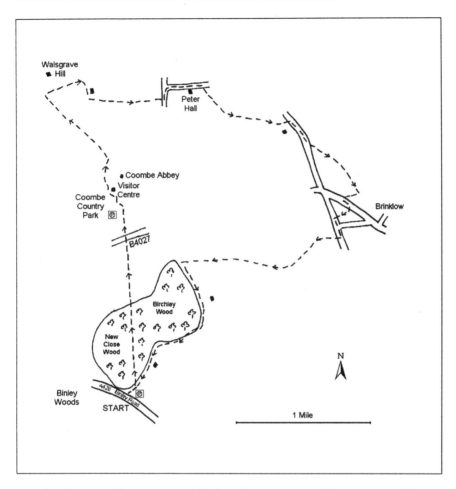

regularly. A well-positioned hide offers memorable views and there are also feeding stations nearby where you can get close to birds in the winter.

Still following the Centenary Way, bear left from the Visitor Centre towards Coombe Pool and then bear right past formal gardens and an arboretum. Pass the end of Top Pool and continue through woodland. After crossing Smite Stream the Centenary Way forks right through more woodland then eventually emerges into arable grassland. Go straight ahead on an unmistakable fenced path. When the fencing comes to an end keep straight on, with a hedge on your right.

Go through a kissing gate and turn right along a farm track which leads to a road. Turn left and then right on Peter Hall Lane. After passing Peter Hall (originally a church, but a farmhouse since the Dissolution in the 16th century) leave the Centenary Way, taking a footpath on the right. Head diagonally left across a field towards an open gateway in a fence. Go forward across two more fields then over a stile into a third. Continue diagonally left past a farm and over a fence in the corner.

Turn right along a road, soon crossing to a "no through road" on the left. Immediately after joining it, climb a stile to a footpath which runs diagonally across a field towards Brinklow. Cross a stile in the far corner into pasture and again go to the far corner. Keep straight on along the edge of the next field, on the Coventry Way. At the far side go over a stile on the right and cross two fields to reach the road on the edge of Brinklow. Turn left, then right on Great Balance. Go straight on past Skipwith Close and George Birch Close, following the street as it bends right.

Join a lane and turn left, ignoring all turnings until you see a footpath sign on the right. Go past a bungalow and along the edge of a garden then over a stile on the left into a large field. Head diagonally across so that you pass just to the right of two ponds. Head initially for the furthest corner of the field, but then aim for a gap in the hedge about 50 metres short of it. Cross a ditch by a slippery footbridge, and then over another field, crossing a track to meet a hedge running on ahead – walk to the left of it, with gravel pits on your left. Continue in the same direction, by the hedge, until you reach a bridleway at the edge of Birchley Wood. Turn left on it and follow it along the edge of the wood, passing Birchley Farm and, eventually, Merton Hall Farm. Continue along the edge of New Close Wood to return to your starting point.

Tea Shop Walks – Spreading everywhere!

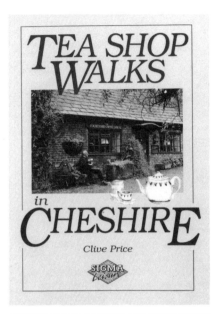

The Sigma Leisure Tea Shop Walks series already includes:

Cheshire

The Chilterns

The Cotswolds

The Lake District, Volume 1

The Lake District, Volume 2

Lancashire

Leicestershire & Rutland

North Devon

The Peak District

Shropshire

Snowdonia

South Devon

Staffordshire

Surrey & Sussex

Warwickshire

The Yorkshire Dales

Each book costs £6.95 and contains an average of 25 excellent walks: far better value than any other competitor!

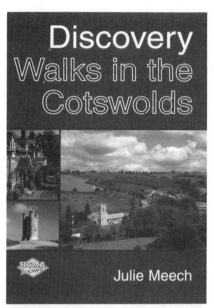

Julie Meech

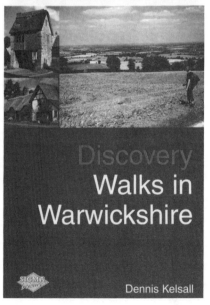

Dennis Kelsall